JER. 6:16

hus saith the Lord,
tand ye in the ways,
nd see, and ask for
he old paths, where
is the good way,
and WALK THEREIN, and
ye shall find rest for
your souls."

Dave Smith

U-gen
edge wear

title page
has bent
corner

writing on
front end page
and back of
title page

DJ has shelf
wear

MEDITATIONS ON

ELIJAH

and

ELISHA

By

TOM WESTWOOD

Published and Distributed
by
THE RALPH E. WELCH FOUNDATION
181 Monterey Road
Orange, California

Gift from:
The Ralph E. Welch Foundation
141 South Center Street
Orange, California
92666
U.S.A.

Gift copies will be furnished upon request.

THE RALPH E. WELCH FOUNDATION
181 Monterey Road
Orange, California

TABLE OF CONTENTS

PART 1. ELIJAH

PART 2. ELISHA

PRINTED IN U.S.A.

PRINTED IN U.S.A. Church Press GLENDALE CALIFORNIA

ELIJAH

The Heavenly Witness

Chapter I

ELIJAH — THE SECRET OF HIS POWER

Among the personalities in the Old Testament Elijah is not the best known although he is one of the most illustrious. He is better known for his exit from life than anything else, for it was he who was caught up to heaven in a chariot of fire.

This last episode of his career, however, is deeply significant of Elijah's entire life and character, for he passes before our view in the sacred pageant of the historical Scriptures as uniquely the man who lived on earth yet belonged to heaven. Keeping this in mind perhaps we may glean from his story much that might be of practical use to us today.

COURAGE IN PUBLIC

His entrance upon the scene in I Kings, chapter 17, finds his world much like our own. They were evil times. The black catalogue of Israel's transgressions had reached an almost unspeakable height. The iniquitous Ahab and the still more wicked Jezebel were king and queen on the throne. The record tells us: "Ahab did more to provoke the Lord God of Israel than all the kings of Israel that were before him." Every spiritual light had been extinguished; every voice for God had been hushed; the spiritual firmament, in which had shone so many luminaries of divine witness, was now overcast with black clouds, and death seemed to lie across the national landscape. It was into this dismal and sorrowful scene that Elijah stepped. He came like a breeze of freshness across a foul and stagnant swamp; like a sudden refreshing shower after a long drought, and not without a storm cloud and an awakening peal of thunder.

COMMUNION IN SECRET

I Kings 17 gives us Elijah's first appearance in public, but the Spirit of God, in James's Epistle in the New Testament, has graciously given us an insight into an earlier episode in his life. The Old Testament historian makes Elijah's entrance abrupt and bold, as he comes with full stride upon the stage of testimony with his alarming shout of "thus saith the Lord." But James gives us the secret of his courage and daring. Without the New Testament record, one might think that he was a kind of "miracle man" who dropped from the heavens much in the same fashion as he went up—in a fiery chariot. But James says: "Elijah was a man subject to like passions as we are, and he prayed earnestly." All too frequently we veil God's servants in Holy Writ with such a halo of mystic smoke that we fail to see in them real men of flesh and blood like ourselves. What then was the secret of this man's power, for it is this which we would ponder.

A RIGHTEOUS INTERCESSOR

James in his Epistle tells us that the effectual, fervent prayer of a righteous man availeth much. The example which he cites is Elijah, who prayed earnestly that it might not rain, and it rained not on the earth for three and a half years. Thus there are initially two things that characterized Elijah's secret life before God that enabled him to come forward with such boldness in public. The two things are: he was a man of *righteousness,* and he was a man of *prayer.* May I suggest that these things ever go together if either has to meet with success.

Whoever would desire to come forward with boldness for God in a world of wickedness must have a background of secret communion with God ere he steps forth. If my position in public testimony exceeds the measure of my secret exercise of soul before God, I shall have cause to tremble, for I shall surely come short. If the superstructure of a building exceed the measure of the foundation below, the building will totter or fall. If a tree shoot forth its branches to a degree exceeding its depths of roots, it will be unequal to the violence of the storm and it will come down. I must be alone *with* God in private as much or more than I am *for* Him in public, else I shall be but a theorist and know not whereof I speak.

It is this secret then that James, in his Epistle, gives us concerning Elijah. That which gave him power and boldness in public was his secret life of righteousness and prayer before his God. His righteousness meant that he came before God not in the merits of his own works but, like Abraham, his faith was counted for righteousness. He knew full well that the wickedness that he witnessed in the world around him found a counterpart in his own heart, and his unworthiness cast him upon the goodness of Jehovah. Having found acceptance for himself and adjustment for his own life before the Lord, then he could become a man of prayer. And the effectual fervent prayer of *that* righteous man availed much.

May I suggest the utter futility of prayer without righteousness. There is no life of communion with God without our first coming into right relations with the God of heaven. Prayers alone will never settle the sin question in our life. The only righteousness that is acceptable before God is the righteousness which is set forth for our acceptation in the person and work of Christ our Redeemer. We find this arresting scripture in the third of Romans: "The righteousness of God which is by faith of Jesus Christ unto all and upon all them that believe." David describes the man to whom God imputes righteousness in this way: "Blessed is the man whose iniquities are forgiven, whose sin is covered." (Rom. 4:6-7.) Our power in public will be commensurate with our life of secret communion with God and never was there a day in which this truth was more needed than now. The world today is in a turmoil of confusion and sorrow.

A MAN OF VISION

Elijah was in tune with God's thoughts concerning a sinful world, and how cheap and tawdry seem the modern religious attitudes compared to the forthright behaviour of this man of God!

He could see the pride and plenty in the world about him. It was evident to him that his people had forgotten God. They no longer assembled to worship Jehovah. A good time was the order of the day. Now I know that modern religious apologists would have told Elijah that he should seek to make religion attractive to the masses. The temple might have been all well and good for King Solomon's time, but things had changed since then, and he must bring the faith of his fathers up to date. But good Elijah had other thoughts! He went to the Lord on his knees, and he asked the Lord to send a drought and a famine. And he prayed earnestly for this. Strange, wasn't it? Elijah knew only too well that only a national calamity would bring the people back to a sense of their dependence upon Jehovah.

But notice what became of Elijah when the drought came. Notice what the Scripture says in 1 Kings 17: "The word of the Lord came to him saying, get thee hence, turn thee eastward, and hide thyself by the brook Cherith, before Jordan. And it shall be, thou shalt drink of the brook, and I have commanded the ravens to feed thee there."

SEPARATION—GET THEE HENCE

How profoundly significant! "Get thee hence; turn eastward; hide thyself." Every Christian should take that to heart. Get thee hence! The Lord says to Elijah: I want you to separate yourself from the evil of the world around you; get away from it! The first essential is separation from evil. Even as Elijah shines so brightly as the heavenly man, so the Christian today in God's thought is a heavenly man also. He is described by Paul in the Ephesian Epistle as "quickened together with Christ, raised up together, and made to sit together in the heavenlies in Christ." "Get thee hence," says the Lord to Elijah, and that is His voice to every Christian. "Set your affections on things above where Christ sitteth." "Your citizenship is in heaven," says Paul. "Ye are not of the world," said our Lord Himself, "even as I am not of the world." *Get thee hence!*

THE BLESSED HOPE—TURN EASTWARD

Then the Lord tells Elijah: *"Turn eastward."* Why look there? Because that is where the sun rises! Turn your back upon the darkness of the night that has enveloped the world about you. In your spirit and your walk move out of it, and have your eye on the eastern sky for a new day is about to dawn. The coming of the Lord draws nigh. Remember Peter's words: "We have also a more sure word of prophecy; whereunto ye do well to take heed, as unto a light that shineth in a dark place, until the day dawn and the day star arise in your hearts." You remember our Lord's final words to us in the closing chapter of the Bible: "I am the root and the offspring of David, the bright and morning star." "He which testifieth these things saith, surely I come quickly. Amen. Even so come Lord Jesus." Turn eastward!

"The Lord Himself shall descend from heaven with a shout, with the voice of the archangel, and with the trump of God; and the dead in Christ shall rise first. Then we which are alive and remain shall be caught up together with them in the clouds to meet the Lord in the air: and so shall we ever be with the Lord." (1 Thess. 4:16-17.) That is the Christian's hope. He is not looking for a better world in the future. He is looking for the Saviour, who will fashion his body of humiliation like unto His own body of glory, and take him into those courts of joy and beauty to be with Him for ever. Yes, turn eastward! The tide of civilization has ever been westward. Man's face is ever towards the sunset, for his glory fades, but the Christian scans the eastern sky for the morning star has risen, and soon the day will dawn for him.

HUMILITY—HIDE THYSELF

"Get thee hence, Elijah," says the Lord, "turn eastward and *hide thyself.*" Oh how we need this last! *"Hide thyself."* We live in a proud and boastful day, but he who would walk true to Jehovah must needs hide himself.

We live in a day when self prominence has beclouded the testimony of the Lord. Perhaps we think there isn't much we can do about it, but we each one for himself can take God's word: "Hide thyself." Perhaps it would make such radical changes in our lives that we cannot face it, but it is God's sure word to Elijah, and it had its rich compensations for him. The Lord says: "You will drink of the brook and I have commanded the ravens to feed thee there."

Envision Elijah that day as he wended his way out from the city, hardly worth notice by the godless throng of merrymakers that filled the highways. Out yonder he went, away from it all! A kind of outcast! He chose a scrubby thicket perhaps out yonder on the desert, hard by the meandering brook. He could hide himself there. And it had a good outlook, for the barren patch fronted towards the eastern sky and his expectations were from the east. There he made his simple camp. No corn field nearby to strengthen his faith in case the Lord forgot him! No, it was desert everywhere. I can imagine him getting up before daylight the first morning to watch the sunrise. And as the sun rose slowly over the horizon the scene about him surely must have looked desolate. Then, in the clear morning light, some black birds started to circle overhead, carrion scavengers no doubt, hoping that he would soon die of starvation and they would pick his bones. But no! They came down close to his camp and, instead of following their natural bent in search of food, they actually dropped food on the rock adjoining, enough for a wholesome breakfast. And each day, morning and night, with the regularity of the sun, the ravens came and left food for Elijah.

The skeptic laughs at the idea, but he who knows God rejoices that He is ever faithful to His word. "I have commanded the ravens to feed thee there." Notice that last word in the text: "I have commanded the ravens to feed thee *there.*" Oh how rich is God's goodness! Elijah did his part; he did as the Lord told him, "get thee hence, turn eastward, and hide thyself by the brook Cherith; thou shalt drink of the brook and I have commanded the ravens to feed thee *there.*"

THE PATH OF HIS WILL

If we but follow in the path of God's will He will never fail us. Sometimes it looks for a while as though God had forgotten, even as it must have looked to Elijah shortly after, when the brook dried up, but he was to learn a still deeper lesson of God's love for him. How much reason we have to be encouraged in reading this story of Elijah! He was a righteous man who prayed earnestly. He was truly a heavenly man who walked the earth in secret with God. Even as Psalm 91 says "He that dwelleth in the secret place of the most high shall abide under the shadow of the Almighty. I will say of the Lord—He is my refuge and my fortress; in Him will I trust. He will cover thee with His feathers and under His wings shalt thou trust." May the Lord give every one of us, His people, to rest more fully in His unfailing love. To any who know Him not as Saviour may I say to you: It is not too late. You may join that happy throng of the redeemed this very hour by simply accepting Christ as your own personal Saviour, and you will be on your way heavenward, just like Elijah, and have the Lord's gracious and unfailing care for you all the way through.

Chapter II

ELIJAH — REFINED AS GOLD

The life story of Elijah brings home to us the importance of the lessons that are learned in secret with God. He who would shine brilliantly in testimony for His Saviour in a wicked world must have a background of experience in secret with his God. The word of the Lord came to Elijah to turn his back upon the world in which he moved, and to wend his way out to the solitary desert in order that God might give him special instruction in the kindly school of His own discipline. He said to Elijah: "Get thee hence, turn eastward, and hide thyself by the brook Cherith, and thou shalt drink of the brook, and I have commanded the ravens to feed thee there." The entire episode is recorded for us in the 17th chapter of 1st Kings, and it is exceedingly fascinating. It indicates a real progression in God's dealings with His servant that is at once both startling and endearing. Let us notice precisely what happens.

This true servant was obedient to the word of the Lord and he made his solitary departure out from the bustle of the city across the plains and into the lonely desert. With precise care he selected his camp hard by the brook as the Lord had told him, and, in that confidence which comes to all of us when we feel that we are definitely in the path of the will of God, he settled down with assurance that almost borders upon the complacent. But one of the direct lessons which Jehovah is going to teach him is that, whatever care the bounteous hand of His Lord may give him, he does not cease to be a pilgrim. Yet see him settling down on the banks of this stream, knowing full well that it was he who had besought the Lord most earnestly to send *a drought*. It had come with its devastating barrenness across the land. I can imagine him saying self-complacently to himself: "Well, those iniquitous people who have forgotten God will soon discover to their dismay that the hand of judgment is upon them." As weeks went into months and no rain fell from the heavens above, he must have said: "No matter how *they* are suffering for their iniquity, here I sit by this brook; I have water to drink, and the ravens come regularly twice a day, and leave food for breakfast and for supper, and I am quite secure."

DEPENDENCE ON GOD

But the Lord would instruct His people that, at no point in our lives, can we ever arrive at a position where He will allow us to cease to be dependent on Him. The Lord will never let us settle down because He knows that this is our real spiritual danger. The moment we cease to have difficulty, the temptation is to become self-complacent and get our eye off our Master.

Then I can imagine Elijah going out one morning at the usual time to receive his breakfast from the ravens that had been commanded by the Lord to feed him, and, as he filled his earthen pitcher from the brook Cherith, he noticed to his dismay that the water level had fallen. He knew full well that the streams throughout the land elsewhere had dried up long ago. It is probable too that he knew that it would be a very long time before rain would come. Now he had relied upon the promise of Jehovah who had told him with great precision just whence his sustenance would come. The ravens would bring him bread and flesh, and the Lord had told him: "Thou shalt drink of the brook Cherith."

Could it be that God was going back on His promise? Surely not! He had never yet trusted Him in vain. I can imagine him watching that brook by the hour, trying to assure himself that the receding of the waters must be on account of some peculiar phenomenon of nature which he had not yet noticed, and that soon the brook again would flow in full tide. But evidences belied his hopes. Day by day the water went lower in the brook. As it receded, the prophet became more and more bewildered. You and I have gone that road, my Christian friend. How often we have walked in a path with the assurance that we were in the will of the Lord and for a time everything worked out splendidly. All circumstances seemed to cordinate to assure our spirits that it was well worth while to walk in obedience to the Lord. Then there came a time when the evidences began to dismay us and we walked the road in bewilderment.

THE WORD "ARISE!"

Think how Elijah must have felt that morning when he came from his grassy couch behind the thicket to discover by the dawn's earliest light that the brook had dried up. We know from Elijah's subsequent history that he was not immune from despondency anyway. I can imagine him sitting down on the banks of what once had been a rippling stream of abundant water, asking himself if, after all, the God he had trusted had failed him. But, as he reflected upon his unhappy plight, he suddenly heard the well-known voice of God Himself. It was the same voice that had said to him: "Get thee hence, turn eastward, hide thyself by the brook and thou shalt drink, and I have commanded the ravens to feed thee." What did it say this time? Here it is in the 9th verse of 1st Kings 17. *"Arise!"* Oh, what a word this is from the Lord Himself! How often it is repeated throughout the Scriptures! This word that has cheered the disconsolate, that has awakened the sleeper, that has made the impotent cripple leap for joy, that has made the bedfast invalid stand up and heave his couch upon his shoulder; yes, a word that has made the dead one come back to life. It is the one word *"arise."* I can see Elijah with great agility jump to his feet as he heard it thunder through the vault of heaven — "Arise" — but what now were his instructions? "Arise, get thee to Zarephath, and dwell there, behold I have commanded a widow woman to sustain thee there. So he arose and went to Zarephath."

Now, to those of us who think that the life of faith is always one of conservative dignity, a Scripture like this must be a great shock, but no more of a shock than it must have been to Elijah on that occasion. It must have seemed to him almost like adding insult to injury. Think what it meant! He had been standing for God in the city giving public witness in a mighty way before multitudes of God-forgetful sinners, and God had told him to get out of there; to go out on the desert, giving him the guarantee that he would have water to drink from the brook and food to eat from the ravens above his head. Yet no sooner had he settled down complacently to enjoy the blessings of the Lord in His care for him day by day than the brook had dried up. That was injury enough, you would think, to the dignity of this servant of the Lord. Now the brook had dried up.

If Elijah had any thought of God finding some dignified way of looking after him, he must have been sadly dismayed when the Lord told him to go to Zarephath and live there because He had commanded a widow to sustain him. Surely it would humiliate any man to be told that he was to be dependent upon a widow for his daily bread. How much more a man like Elijah who had been so faithful to the Lord and was, I suppose, in his own estimation, deserving of so much! However, God was going to teach him an outstanding lesson and that was that there was one thing of importance in his life—obedience to his Lord. In order to serve

God aright he must be emptied of himself and this was the process through which Jehovah was putting him to that end.

SEPARATION

Now notice the very interesting meaning of the two words. The name of the brook "Cherith" and the place where this widow woman was located. The words are exceedingly interesting. "Cherith" means "separation." God was teaching him at Cherith that he should be dependent only on the Lord, not with the dignity of any claim that he personally had upon Jehovah, but in separation from the wicked ways of the world around him. There is a path here on earth for every man that is well pleasing to God. It is the path that Job describes in his 28th chapter. It is a path of wisdom; it is also a path of suffering and, more than anything else, it is a path of separation from the world. No one can walk well-pleasing to the Lord in this day and age, or in any other, until he is delivered in his soul from the noxious influences of a world away from God. And this is the lesson that God taught Elijah by the brook Cherith, which means "separation."

But now this word "Zarephath" has a very interesting meaning also. It means "a place where gold is refined." Yes, God would teach His servant more than separation from this world. He would teach him further that he is not his own, that his body and spirit belong to God, and that the gold of the handiwork of Jehovah which is in his soul, must be refined before he is well-pleasing to God. When the Lord Himself refers to this incident in the 4th chapter of Luke, he uses the word Sarepta instead of this word Zarephath, and I was interested to see that the meaning of the word Sarepta is "a goldsmith's shop." Let us linger upon this thought for a moment, because it might speak encouragement to many of God's people.

God would conduct our souls into that place where He refines gold. I note the Apostle Peter's words in this connection in the 1st chapter of his 1st Epistle: "That the trial of your faith being much more precious than of gold that perisheth, though it be tried with fire, might be found unto praise and honor and glory at the appearing of Jesus Christ." And again in his 4th chapter, Peter says: "Beloved, think it not strange concerning the fiery trial which is to try you, as though some strange thing happened unto you. But rejoice inasmuch as ye are partakers of Christ's sufferings; that, when His glory shall be revealed ye may be glad also with exceeding joy."

THE GOLDSMITH'S ART

This then, is the Christian's "Zarephath," the place where gold is refined. Only too well the Lord knows that there is much dross in your life and mine, and He must take us to the place where gold is refined, that we might be emptied of self. Not that we should be needlessly humiliated, but that we should learn the good lesson that we cannot lean upon anything that we are or have, but that our confidence alone must be in Jehovah. Yes, this is Sarepta, "the goldsmith's shop," and I like to think that the Lord as a master goldsmith is not needlessly applying the fiery trial, but, with divinely measured mercy and wisdom, He is putting us through those processes of difficulty in order that we might come out of them purified, made strong, and fashioned more according to the glory of the One in whose likeness we are yet to shine. This is the goldsmith's art. A Christian is a vessel in His hand, which by fiery trial is being made more and more conformed to His image, being purged of the dross of self of this world, being separated day by day from the evil in order that this enduring substance called "gold," the handiwork of the Lord in our soul, might shine with undimmed brilliance in the day of glory.

The Christian is marked by God Himself for a glorious destiny, to be conformed to the image of His Son, to be a living stone in that magnificent structure of gold which shall come forth in dazzling brightness and beauty as "a bride adorned for her husband." But it is now that we are taking on the color and true brilliance in which we will shine in the undimmed glory of that day. Let us then be more like Elijah, who went with willing footsteps in obedience to the Lord, turning his back now upon a dried-up brook that had once meant the sustenance of his life, to wend his way downward to this distant city where he was to be dependent upon a destitute widow. It is when the skies are dark, when circumstances seem to be all against us, when prospects are naturally the most dismal, that is the place where gold is refined. That is our "Sarepta."

It is well for us to remind ourselves of what Peter says in his Epistle in this same connection that "the spirit of glory rests upon us." I like to think that every Christian man and woman on this earth has the mark of destiny upon him. No matter how we may mingle with the worldlings, no matter how hard we try to run with the common herd, yet God has marked us with the destiny of His own purpose and grace. Our names are enregistered in heaven. God has said: "These shall be mine in the day that I make up my jewels." We get the grand truth in golden letters in the 8th chapter of Romans. "We know that all things work together for good to them that love God, to them who are the called according to his purpose; for whom He did foreknow, He also did predestinate to be conformed to the image of His Son that He might be the first-born among many brethren. What shall we then say to these things, if God be for us, who can be against us?"

A LIFE OF THRIUMPH

Christianity is a life of triumph because it is the life of the risen Christ. If you are a believer on the Lord Jesus Christ, God has marked you for endless bliss. God's call to Elijah is His call to you and me: "Get thee hence, turn eastward, hide thyself by the brook." If the brook fails, there is no need to sit down in despondency. God again says to us: "Arise, get thee to Zarephath," the place where gold is refined, and you can rely upon God even there, although the prospects of dependence upon a destitute widow are the most meager imaginable.

Chapter III

ELIJAH — GUEST AND BENEFACTOR

We have been considering together the fascinating story of the experiences of Elijah, the prophet, as recorded for us in 1st Kings, chapter 17. We observe the personal exercises of this great servant of God, and the way these exercises molded him as a man of faith. The incident which shall occupy our attention now brings him before us as one of the most striking types of our Lord Himself in the entire Old Testament.

Elijah had been directed by the Lord to leave the city behind, and to go out and hide himself in solitude by the brook, where he should have water to drink, and where the ravens would come twice a day to feed him according to the Lord's commandment. We saw how the brook dried up, much to the dismay of the Prophet, and the voice of the Lord directed him to arise and go down into the Gentile country to Zaraphath and dwell there: "Behold," said the Lord, "I have commanded a widow woman there to sustain thee."

The scene is very graphically depicted for us and I like to think that we in this age have a grandstand seat to watch this impelling drama enacted before us on the stage of long ago. I imagine I see Elijah that day taking a last lingering look at the dried-up brook. It had for a long time been the token for him of Jehovah's care, and a constant reminder to his soul that, although the entire land lay under the sweltering curse of a three and a half years' drought, yet he always had the flowing stream of the brook Cherith. "The secret of the Lord is with them that fear Him," and truly enough this trickling brook in the midst of a great barren desert had been the secret of the Lord to Elijah and had meant his very life. Now it was as arid as the wilderness about him and he turns his back upon it and goes, with trembling steps perhaps, but still in obedience to the word of Jehovah, down across the plains, beyond Israel's borders, until he comes into the country of Zidon, the Gentile country, native land of the wicked queen Jezebel.

A GENTILE WIDOW

Every mile of his journey was a grim reminder to him of the devastation which had been brought upon the land in answer to his own prayer, for it was he who had earnestly prayed that the Lord should send a drought and a famine. Was he now to be caught in the mesn of his own mistaken desires and die in the wilderness? But he covered the distance all right and I see him in the kindly morning light, after a weary journey, find his solitary way toward the approaches of this Gentile town called Zarephath. What misgivings must have filled his mind! All the Lord had told him was that He had commanded a widow to sustain him there. There was no indication as to who she was, or in what circumstances she might be found. Inasmuch as the New Testament Scripture reminds us that Elijah was a man of like passions with ourselves, no doubt he conjured up in his fertile imagination a vivid picture of the well-to-do lady, amply provided-for in a palatial mansion, and with whom he would be housed with the greatest of opulence. Yet, as he approaches the city gates, the first thing that greets his eye is a woman as lonely as himself. Her widow weeds proclaim to him at once that she has no husband, she is a widow. Could this be the woman of his search? Everything about her bespeaks poverty and she is groveling in the sand in no-man's land outside the city gates trying to salvage a few scraps of firewood. This *surely* could not be God's widow upon whom he is yet to be dependent for his daily bread!

BREAD AND WATER

Yet there is one thing about a man of faith that outstrips all others. He is not guided simply by evidences. The possibility that this might be the lady in spite of her poverty-stricken appearance encourages Elijah to make a venture. He asks her for a drink of water and I suppose he must have been very thirsty. Her response to his request encourages him and, as he sees her go off to fetch the water, he thinks he'll try going a little further. He says: "Bring me, I pray thee, a morsel of bread in thine hand." Bread and water! His demands were certainly very simple, but how astonished he must have been at her reply. She turns round to him and her words are very significant. "As the Lord, thy God liveth." What? A Gentile woman speaks of "the Lord thy God." "I have not a cake, but an handful of meal in a barrel and a little oil in a cruse, and behold I am gathering two sticks that I might go in and dress it for me and my son, that we may eat and die."

If we ever think that our outlook upon life is black, we should think well of Elijah on this occasion. I am much inclined to think that, even although he had a great deal of experience in the faithfulness of the Lord, his heart must have sunk. For abject poverty, the condition of this widow could hardly be equalled anywhere. How then was she going to be able to sustain herself, her son and a boarder besides? Whatever misgivings Elijah may have had, his trust in the Lord was not shaken. He who knows the omnipotence of the Almighty knows that man's extremity is God's opportunity.

Notice what Elijah says to this poor widow. *"Fear not."* What words are these! "Go and do as thou hast said, for thus saith the Lord God of Israel. The barrel of meal shall not waste, neither shall the cruse of oil fail, until the day that the Lord sendeth rain upon the earth." Let us write down that verse of 1st Kings, 17:14, in our memory book, and, when days are dark and prospects are at their blackest, remember the word of the Lord through Elijah: "The barrel of meal shall not waste, neither shall the cruse of oil fail, until the day that the Lord sendeth rain upon the earth." Yes, God shall never fail his people! Days of anguish and sorrow, turmoil and confusion; war and upheaval may come along, yet Jehovah is on the Throne. He who makes God his trust, he that believeth, shall never be confounded.

THE BARREL AND CRUSE

According to God's promise to the Gentile woman through Elijah, she had faith enough to take God at His word. She reached her long and bony arm into the almost empty barrel, scraping up the scanty remnants of meal in the bottom to knead a cake for the prophet. For some mysterious reason, although she poured a little oil out of the cruse that stood yonder in the corner well-nigh empty for so long, yet there was still a little left in it. In spite of all her scraping at the bottom of the barrel, somehow there always remained a handful of meal there. Surely it would have been just as easy for Jehovah to have filled up the barrel, and filled up the cruse, and set this widow with her son and her boarder, Elijah, perfectly at their ease, but methinks the Lord knows us all too well for anything like that. Although He sunstained them by His mighty power, He ever kept them on the very edge of the possibility of want that they might always keep their trust in Him.

How easy it would be for the Lord to ease our circumstances, to take away our difficulties, to fill up our barrel and our cruse; to change the whole picture of our life and take away all our fears and worries. Why doesn't He do it? It is because the Lord wants to keep us in the attitude of dependence upon Himself; because *there* only are we kept in safety. It is when we become independent and self-sufficient that the enemy of our souls finds a vulnerable point of attack and we become proud and overbearing, and of little service to the Lord. As long as there is just a *handful* of meal in the barrel and just a *little* oil in the cruse, how natural it is for us to look up to heaven above and say to our Lord: "Give us *this* day our daily bread."

That is the picture we have here in Elijah and the widow woman in 1st Kings 17. True to the word of Jehovah, the barrel never became empty, nor did the cruse of oil ever fail, until the drought and the famine were over and rain fell upon the earth. The Lord's care for us will never terminate until the rain comes. What rain? The rain the Psalmist wrote about in the 72nd Psalm when he said. "He shall come down like rain upon the mown grass, as showers that water the earth. In His days shall the righteous flourish; and abundance of peace so long as the moon endureth. He shall have dominion also from sea to sea, and from the river unto the ends of the earth." Yes, the rain is coming for our Lord is coming! "He shall come down like showers upon the new-mown grass, and joy and hope like flowers, spring up where He doth pass." Oh, what a blessed hope this is! It is God's unquestioned guarantee that, until the Lord comes to take us home, the Lord's care and provision for His people will be unfailing.

THE RESURRECTION

A very interesting episode follows which is worthy of our note. No sooner do these three, Elijah, the widow, and her son, settle down to indulge sparingly, but with gratitude, in the sustenance of the Lord's providing, than suddenly another unexpected calamity befalls the little household. "Will the skies never clear?" they must have asked. The boy in the home "fell sick and his sickness was so sore that there was no breath left in him." This was too much for the widow. The one upon whom she could look naturally for help, her only boy, has been taken from her. You can hardly blame the bereaved mother for looking questioningly at Elijah, and attributing this calamity largely to his presence in her home, or as a mark of Jehovah's displeasure. But the man of faith is again equal to the occasion. He looks at the dejected widow, as she embraced the lifeless body of her only child, and he picks him up and carries him up into the loft where he abode, and lays him upon his own bed.

Note this incidental information concerning Elijah; he abode in the loft. However great a prophet he might have been, he was a very humble man, and the Spirit of God makes note of this in intimating to us that Elijah didn't live in the best room in the house. He was not the kind of man to take over the best bedroom. He slept in the loft. Elijah takes the lad up and puts him on his own bed, stretches himself upon the child three times and prays the Lord for his revival. Miraculously the boy is resurrected and restored to his mother who says to Elijah: "Now by this I know that thou art a man of God, and that the word of the Lord in thy mouth is truth."

TYPE OF CHRIST

In all of this we have Elijah shining as a wonderful type of our Lord and Saviour, Jesus Christ Himself. You will notice the setting of the whole episode from first to last. Elijah has turned his back upon a dried-up brook in the land of Israel, and gone down among the Gentiles to find this destitute widow woman. In this there is a beautiful picture of Christ Himself who, after he was refused by Israel's race, and the brook from which he properly expected to receive refreshment dried up, turned to the Gentiles. "He came unto His own and His own received Him not. But to as many as received Him, to them gave He the power to become the children of God, even to them that believe on His name" (John 1:11-12). That is the picture in antitype. Christ turns his back upon Israel. He comes down among the Gentiles, but he finds destitution there, and poverty and death. It was while *we* were yet without strength that Christ died for the ungodly. What a graphic picture we have of the Gentile sinner in this widow woman! Gathering sticks to cook her last meal before she and her offspring should die. This expresses our condition most fully.

PROVIDER AND LIFE GIVER

This widow woman learned Elijah in two different ways, even as we may learn our Lord Jesus Christ. She learned that Elijah, although seeming to be dependent upon her, and finding comfort in her companionship, actually became her sustainer. Without Elijah, the meal would have given out; without him the cruse of oil would have failed, and she and her son would have died. Thus, in every department of her life, she was absolutely dependent upon Elijah. But more than this, she found that he who had the power to bring the sustenance into her daily life, also had the power to raise the dead. That is the grandest aspect in which we can see our Lord Himself. He it is alone who can meet our need here and now, but He is the One who could say: "I am the resurrection and the life, he that believeth on Me, though he were dead, yet shall he live, and he that liveth and believeth on Me shall never die" (John 11:25-26).

This is the antitype of Elijah; this is what we have in our Lord Jesus Christ. Just as Elijah laid himself upon the child face to face, so identifying himself completely with his impotence and his death, even so our Lord Himself has identified Himself with you and me, for He "was made sin for us who knew no sin." Jehovah laid on him the iniquities of us all. On Calvary's Cross He took our place. Just as Elijah repeated this performance three times over before the child came to life, so our Lord Himself, in becoming the sin-bearer, died, was buried, and on the third day He rose from the dead.

I wonder if the reader has been brought into living touch with the antitype of Elijah, the One who can make the widow's heart rejoice; the One who has power to see that the barrel of meal will never waste and the cruse of oil will never fail; the One, too, who is the Risen Man, who said: "He that believeth on Me, though He were dead, yet shall he live." As natural men in this world we are dead in trespasses and in sins, and we need the quickening voice of the Lord Jesus to bring us into new life. He said "Verily, verily I say unto you, the hour is coming and now is, when the dead shall hear the voice of the Son of God, and they that hear shall live" (John 5:25). This is the glorious truth of the Gospel, and it is offered for the acceptance of every one.

Chapter IV

ELIJAH — A SHINING WITNESS

We now come to another meditation on the life and experiences of God's servant of the Old Testament, Elijah, the Prophet. We have seen the exercises and the occupation of this remarkable man of God from the time he looked upon the wickedness which characterized his people, Israel, in that day. He prayed the Lord to withhold the rain and send a famine that they might be brought to their senses. The famine came and, for three and a half long years, anxious faces scanned the heavens in vain for signs of moisture. The azure blue of a cloudless sky, day after day, month after month, was the monotonous aspect while Elijah himself nestled securely under the feathered wing of Jehovah's care. Encamped by the rippling brook and fed by ravens night and morning, the Lord sustained the Prophet; and when the brook dried up, the man of God found haven at the scanty board of a poor Gentile woman, where, through the Lord's measured goodness the barrel of meal wasted not, neither did the cruse of oil fail.

In the opening of the 18th chapter of 1st Kings, three years of drought and famine had run their course and the word of the Lord comes to Elijah saying: "Go show thyself unto Ahab." Three years before the word of Jehovah to him had been: "Go hide thyself." Now it is: "Go show thyself." It is a reminder to us all that he who would come out in public witness for his Lord must first have learned the humility of self-effacement. It is the holy priest who is seen going into the sanctuary with God who comes out as the royal priest to show forth the graces of Him who has called him out of darkness into His marvelous light. (1 Peter 2.)

In this 18th chapter of 1st Kings, there are three men who are brought before us, and they are exceedingly interesting. I should like to sketch a word picture of all three of them that we each might see clearly our own reflection in one of three. I believe these three men display in their characteristics the entire range of humanity as God sees us here in this world. Elijah is the one who shines the brightest, but there are two others. One is Ahab, the King of Israel, and the third is Obadiah, a God-fearing courtier of prominence in the King's household.

Of Elijah himself we need say little. He was a man of God

from start to finish. There was not a vestige of compromise in his whole makeup; he was one who could turn his back upon the world, not because he disliked humanity, but because he was living in an age when men had turned away from his Lord, and he found that he had no part in their evil ways. He chose a path of separation, even as our Lord Himself has indicated for every Christian who is staunch-hearted in his affection for Christ. He has said of us: "They are not of the world, even as I am not of the world." Our Lord has indicated to those who would be faithful to Him that the world would hate them even as it hated Him. Elijah had accepted the truth of this, and his life's journey was planned accordingly. His footsteps carried him beyond the glamour and tinsel of a make-believe world, away from the idolatry of covetousness and man-made gods. He preferred the company of His Lord by the lonely brook or across the parched desert, or in the humble dwelling of a poor widow in his little room in the attic.

Elijah was no recluse whose shyness or inferiority complex drove him from the haunts of men. On the contrary, he was a bold and fearless servant of God who could denounce the King on his royal throne with as little compunction as he would ask a drink of water from a widow. Elijah was neither stoic nor human pervert, but a real, down-to-earth man of deep conviction and courageous testimony who chose, like many another of God's people, a path of reproach and suffering rather than join hands with the world to enjoy its transient and vaporous pleasures of sin for a season.

THE FALSE PROFESSOR

In contrast to Elijah, the man of God, we have Ahab, the King. He was a wicked man who was married to a still more wicked woman. He moved in a sphere of rebellion against his God. In his hand was the scepter of Israel's honor. He was the ruler of God's chosen people, Israel. He occupied a throne whereon had sat men like David, whose loyalty to the Lord was the brightest gem in his kingly crown. On that same throne had sat Solomon in all his glory, transcendent in splendor and in wisdom, yet Ahab had laid all of that in the dust and confusion of God-forgetfulness. His epitaph is written in letters of the darkest shame in the 16th chapter of this same book: "And Ahab did evil in the sight of the Lord above all that were before him."

What a distinction! This, then, is the second of these three who come before our notice in 1st Kings 18. And what a contrast this man Ahab presents against the colorful and entrancing background of the story of Elijah, God's faithful witness!

ON DAVID'S THRONE

As King of Israel, Ahab was professedly the leader of his people. Had he read the story of his predecessor David, he would have found these words: "The God of Israel said: the Rock of Israel spake to me, He that ruleth over men must be just, ruling in the fear of God." (2 Samuel 23:3.) But Ahab was a traitor to his position. His profession was false; he was a man in high religious place, but his heart was corrupt. May I suggest that he has his counterpart in many of us here in the world this very hour? Never was there a day when religious profession has reached such an acme of splendor as it has today. Yet in spite of all our profession, the vast majority of those who have set their hand and seal to the name of "Christian" are unregenerate in heart with little or no thought of God in their lives. He had taken a position of respectability and honor. Every head in the land looked up to the throne on which he sat. As he passed in the street, the people would bow before him, yet the moral springs of his being were foul and polluted. He had a name to live and he was dead. It is well for every one of us to mirror ourselves against this picture of Ahab. There are thousands in our fair land today who pass under the name of Christian. Their names may have been signed to some church register; they are held in high repute, perhaps, by those around them; a fair percentage of their income goes for the good cause of Christ's Kingdom, yet their sins have never been forgiven for His Name's sake.

If that is your case, my friend, look well at Ahab! He had all the gaudy trappings of religious office. Not a man in the land, except Elijah, could call him in question. Yet the day was to come when he would stand in abject self-abasement before the pronounced judgment of this same man of God. It may be that you or I have not sunk to the depths of iniquity of which Ahab was guilty, but the great point at issue with this man Ahab was that he was false to his profession. He pretended to be what he was not. David's inspired words had told him that he that ruleth men must be just, ruling in the fear of God. Yet the secrets of his own heart would have told him that he was not that man.

THE WORLDLY CHRISTIAN

But there is a third man in this chapter and his name is Obadiah. He was a man who wanted all the advantages of Godliness, but wanted also to stay on at the court of the wicked King. He was outstandingly a man of compromise. He refused to separate himself from the world. His motto was convenience, and he thought he could live for God in the sphere in which his lot was cast no matter where that might be. He is a picture of the Christian who is living in the world, who has never yet come into the light of his association with Christ in the realm outside the sphere of things here. He was somewhat like Jonathan who loved David in his heart, intensely attached to the person of David, yet unwilling to turn his back upon the court of Saul and take the lonely road that went out to the cave of Adullam to share the affliction and privation of David's rejection.

So Obadiah stayed on as lord over the house of Ahab, the wicked King.

While Elijah was sitting in his lonely attic down yonder in the Gentile country in the widow's home, Obadiah was revelling in the entertainment and excitement of the King's palace. While Elijah was eating sparingly of the scanty fare of meal from the barrel and oil from the cruse, Obadiah was feasting sumptuously no doubt on the luscious delicacies under the sneering eye of Jezebel in the royal household. He was a God-fearing man who couuld put his testimony in his pocket when the occasion suited, yet boasted of the fact that his faithfulness to God had given sanctuary to a hundred prophets who were fleeing for their lives and whom he hid by fifties in a cave.

Let us notice the particular occupation of Obadiah in this chapter. It is quite arresting. Now that the drought had lasted about three years, the land was parched and dry, and the record here indicates two figures in ludicrous dignity, Ahab, the king, and Obadiah his henchman, going through the length and breadth of the land, searching for grass! Their carnal minds were much more occupied with the salvation of a few mules and horses than with the salvation of Israel. They were more concerned about finding fodder for dumb animals than bringing relief to the starving thousands of their people. I can see these two men running here and there, in confused anxiety, looking for waterholes where they might find a little grass for their horses. What an anti-climax to their wicked revelry in the royal palace!

One can readily understand Ahab the King, because he had no knowledge of God in his heart, but Obadiah is the pathetic figure. He it is who should have had the courage to say to Ahab, that if he would only turn to God and forsake the wickedness of his way, God himself would bring about relief. But Obadiah was too cowardly for that. He would rather run hand in hand with the King on a fruitless escapade of grass hunting than kneel down in contrition and repentance before God. He would rather search the land for waterholes than look to heaven for abundance of rain. He is an emblem of the worldly Christian. His eyes are downward instead of upward. He refuses to concede that the Lord's words are true: "Ye are not of the world even as I am not of the world." He refuses the Scripture: "Set your affection upon things above, not on things on the earth." He is, like Obadiah, still looking in this world for green spots where grass may grow, unwilling to concede that the rejection of Christ has left this world a barren wilderness. Like Obadiah, on horseback, in company with the false and perfidious King Ahab, going through the land hoping to find some remnant of hope for the recovery of the world without God's intervention, the worldly Christian today is on an equally futile hunt.

Thus we have these three men in this chapter. Ahab, the unregenerate and wicked King, who has assumed a place of false profession enshrined in fading glory; Obadiah, the man who at heart belonged to the Lord, yet did not have the courage to step forth and separate himself from the world, seeking rather to improve it without God; and then Elijah, the magnificent—the man who put his faith above expediency, who was prepared to tread a path of loneliness and rejection in dependence upon His God rather than mix in a world where his Lord had been rejected.

Now notice one more verse in this chapter, 1st Kings 18, where these two men meet face to face. It is this: "And as Obadiah was in the way, behold Elijah met him and he knew him and fell on his face and said, art thou *my lord* Elijah. And Elijah answered, I am, go tell *thy lord,* behold *Elijah* is here." There we get the proper order. The real cause of Obadiah's failure is found here. King Ahab, you see, was lord to Obadiah. Woe betide the Christian who allows the devil's world to have the ascendancy over Christ in his soul. But as Obadiah stands face to face with Elijah, who is God's man, the man who is faithful to the testimony of his Lord, then Obadiah falls on his face and he says: "Art thou *my Lord, Elijah.*" The carnal Christian will eventually look up to the heavenly man. The man who has made the reproach of Christ his choice is held in high honor by the man who compromises with the world.

Thus we have in this chapter the man who makes a profession with no possession, his name is Ahab; Obadiah, the carnal Christian, the man whose heart belongs to the Lord, but who does not have the courage to be true to Him; and Elijah the heavenly man, who esteems the reproach of Christ greater riches than Egypt's treasure. May God give us each one to be true to our profession!

Chapter V

ELIJAH ON MOUNT CARMEL

We see Elijah, in the 18th chapter of 1st Kings, returning from three years of secluded retirement to take his stand before the wicked King Ahab. We watch him in obedience to the word of the Lord wend his way out across the desert to make his humble camp by the brook Cherith, to be fed under the care of the Almighty by the ravens that came night and morning to his camp. The brook having dried up, we see him descend to the Gentile country, and now housed in the humble home of a destitute widow, where he abides in quiet retirement while drought and famine rage throughout the land.

Here, in 1st Kings 18, again at the bidding of Jehovah, he is coming out of retirement to stand before Ahab, the King. Obadiah, the man who had feared God from his youth up, but who had been too cowardly to bear testimony to his faith, is fittingly enough the first to meet Elijah on his way toward the city. As he sees the venerable prophet making his approach, Obadiah abases himself before him even as the Christian today who goes hand in hand with the world finds himself dwarfed in the presence of the uncompromising godliness of a fellow-believer who is loyal to Christ. It is a marvelous object lesson to us all in the dignity of Christian loyalty. Obadiah is sent by Elijah as a messenger to his lord and master, the wicked Ahab, to make the grand announcement—*"behold Elijah is here."*

Evidently they had searched the land high and low for Elijah. Undoubtedly his courage and his piety had made him a marked man in those wicked days. When he suddenly vanished from sight, rumor went wild as to his whereabouts. He was reported here, then there. Before his presence could be properly investigated, he was gone, and Obadiah is terrified that, before his unworthy feet will carry him to Ahab's palace, Elijah may again vanish and he will be slain for his perfidy. But Elijah assures him that he will be there.

Now Ahab, the king, comes out to meet Elijah. What a meeting that must have been! The man who had been the arch conspirator in every ungodly device in the land, who had led his people, Israel, into more evil than all who had been before him, stands face to face with Elijah, the Prophet, whose towering personality must have dwarfed him in the dust of shame and humiliation. Ahab exclaims in astonishment: "Art thou he that troubleth Israel?"

How like a wicked man of the world! When he sees that, in the heyday of his career of evil, everything goes awry, he is sure to blame his calamity either upon God himself or upon one of His servants. It had been Elijah that had warned the people to turn from their idolatry to the God of Israel, and his prayers on their behalf had been heard in the courts of heaven itself, yet it is Elijah who is blamed for the catastrophe into which the nation has been plunged through the wickedness of Ahab, the King, the treachery of his queen, Jezebel, and the idolatry of his people.

In that day of long ago they blamed Elijah, the man who alone had the power and the wisdom to direct the nation in a path of honor and blessing. Yet it has its counterpart in every era. There are those around us who are all too ready to blame catastrophe upon God Himself and His Christ. In our individual lives as well as in things national and international, the wicked schemes of unscrupulous men so often drag us into the morass of difficulty and despair and we turn around glibly enough and ask why God allows all of this. Oh that we each would look into our own hearts for the answer!

THE WORLD'S BLAME

It is two thousand years since God's servant, Jesus Christ our Lord was here in this world, proclaiming to all mankind a way out of all difficulty. At His birth the Angels announced "Glory to God in the highest; on earth peace; good will towards men." But the sweet melody of the herald's voice had hardly stilled across the dark Judean hills when the cold hand of rejection was felt by the babe of Bethlehem's manger. Men said: "No room for Him in the inn." Among the cattle was His place. Nor did the attitude improve with time. As Jesus grew up in the city of Nazareth and slowly reached the years of His manhood to step forth in public testimony as to who He was, His own people, Israel, rejected Him. Those who should have received Him gladly departed from Him. They heaped upon Him derision as their voices blended with their own taskmasters, the Romans, to shout "Away with Him, crucify Him, we will not have this Man to reign over us." From that day to this, throughout these twenty centuries, the black shadow of the rejection of Christ has lain like a pall of darkness upon all creation. Yet still men blame God for the calamitous ways in which their wickedness leads them. It is all but the re-echo of Ahab's words: "Art thou he that troubleth Israel?"

Sure enough man's extremity is God's opportunity. As Elijah looks into the care-worn eyes of Ahab, the King, his spirit rises to the dignity of his calling. He first denounces the wicked monarch and his father's house because they have forsaken the commandments of the Lord and have gone into idolatry; and then he announces to Ahab, the King, that there is going to be a gala day in the land. Ahab may be officially the King, but it is Elijah, the Prophet, God's man, in this hour of extremity who is giving the commands. Things have got out of hand. The people are starving. There is no prospect of rain in the heavens. Ahab and his henchman, Obadiah, have traversed the land from north to south, and east to west, searching for grass for the dumb animals and they have found none. They have tried their own way to the limit and it has failed. Now the voice of Elijah must be heard, and he announces a most astonishing event.

It is going to be a kind of carnival. Mt. Carmel will be the location. Elijah's word is: "All Israel shall be gathered together on Mt. Carmel." For good measure the King is told that he must bring four hundred and fifty of the prophets of Baal, a veritable horde of false deceivers that had attached themselves like so many parasites to Queen Jezebel, feeding constantly from the bounty of her table. Now they are all to be assembled on Mt. Carmel. Elijah is going to decide this matter once and forever. The quesion of idolatry is not a light one. It will be put publicly to the test.

A CARNIVAL SETTING

I think it must have had, as I say, the aspect of a mammoth carnival as the people trooped by the thousands from the city across the barren and withered fields, across the desert, and up the slopes of this great mountain, all to be assembled there on the mountain top to witness one of the greatest spectacles that human eyes had ever beheld. All those wicked men who had made such a mark in the revelry of the city life, they were there. Men, women and children by the thousands made the long trek. I can see the motley throng marching in somewhat gleeful disorder, their hearts filled with expectation of something, they knew not what. These few hundred prophets of Baal must have had strange foreboding as they ambled along in the procession, wondering what surprise Elijah was going to present. They knew all the trickery of their idolatrous business, and they were well aware that they had deceived the people with skill and with elegance, but never yet had they seen a man who could command the whole nation to gather together in one spot and find them coming from every direction at his command, marching toward the Mount called Carmel.

And they were not all wicked men that journeyed thither. The Lord intimates to us in the record later, that there were some seven thousand of these same people who secretly in their hearts were loyal to the Lord, and whose knees had never bent to the false god. They were lost in the crowd, surely, but I like to think that their hearts danced for very joy as they kept their eyes upon Elijah, and they marched onward feeling that their moment was now coming. They had been like stars in a firmament totally beclouded by the fogs of idolatrous wickedness awaiting a more brilliant light than their own to dispel these fogs so that they might also shine forth. Their light had now come in Elijah, and they were with him in heart although they lacked courage to be by his side. But Elijah hardly needed them, for he walked in that quiet confidence which comes to every believer who senses that God is for him, and says, like the Apostle Paul, the champion of the faith in the New Testament—"If God be for us, who can be against us?"

So we envision Elijah as he marched before this great mixed company, out across the plains and up the sunny slopes of the mountain to stage a demonstration that would settle once and for all as to whether there was anything to this matter of being faithful to God. It was going to be rather an unequal combat from the human point of view. Publicly Elijah was going to stand alone for God because there was no other man of God with courage enough to take his place by his side. By special invitation, however, Elijah had made sure that the opposing camp would be well represented. Four hundred and fifty of the prophets of Baal were going to take their stand against one man. How fearless was the man of God!

Having reached Carmel's sunny heights he steps forth before the multitude of people, and he declares to them very clearly that the day of compromise is over forever. A crucial moment has arrived when men must make a decision. Their famine ridden lives depend upon it. He says: "How long will ye halt between two opinions? If Jehovah be God, follow Him; and if Baal, then follow him." And the people answered him not a word. How that challenge must have run through the camp as Elijah stood there in the solitary dignity of his godliness, declaring that he was the only public witness for the Lord, His God, and that Baal had four hundred and fifty prophets there to represent *him.*

This is the fearlessness of Christian confidence. The world has nothing to match it and it is most admirable at all times. The Christian may often seem feeble and somewhat unworthy in the estimation of the world around, but, when a crisis arrives, it is the Christian who shines with true lustre even as Elijah did on this occasion. The Christian is the only one in the world today who can be sure of anything. The worldling knows nothing for certain. His pleasures are fleeting like the winds; his opinions change like a weathervane; he has no tomorrow to which he can look forward with any degree of certainty. The Christian, on the other hand, can say with the Apostle Paul: "I know whom I have believed, and am persuaded that He is able to keep that which I have committed unto Him against that day." Elijah, here in 1st Kings 18, stands face to face with these false prophets, and he knows full well that he on the Victor's side and that he will put them all to shame.

Now an altar is set up, a bullock is chosen, and dressed, and put upon the altar, and the contest will be to discover which of the gods, either Baal or Jehovah Himself will be able to send the fire that will consume the bullock. The stage is dramatically set here in this convenient amphitheatre on Mt. Carmel, where the thousands of spectators can watch with avid interest the result. From morning till noon-day these false prophets work themselves into a veritable frenzy of mock piety, calling upon their idols to send fire for the sacrifice. They cut themselves with stones, they drew blood all over their bodies to demonstrate the zeal with which they believed in their gods, but all to no avail. No fire comes! Their zealous ardor turns into violent rage and Elijah stands quietly by, watching their confusion. There are seven thousand hearts in that great crowd that leap in ecstasy at their idolatrous failure and a hallelujah echoes through their souls. The false prophets howl and rage in their confusion. They jump upon the altar and pull it to pieces and then retire in abashed humiliation.

Watch the next performer! Elijah steps to the front. I can see him in the dignity of his confidence. The first thing he does is that he personally clears away the idolatrous rubbish and he rebuilds the altar. Oh, how needful it is for all of us to realize in the confusion of our God-forgetfulness, this is our first necessity! God's altar has been torn to pieces. It takes an Elijah to rebuild it. But not until the altar is rebuilt will the people be brought back to God. Elijah knows this very well and, more than this, he gathers together twelve stones and sets them up in the midst of the multitude as a reminder to them of the princely position in which Israel was set by God Himself. He reminds them that they are still twelve tribes and that they are sprung from one whose name is not merely Jacob, but Israel, "a prince with God."

Surely many of these tribes had already been scattered and there was little semblance in this confused company to the host of the Lord which had subsisted in such wonderful order in the days before their dispersion. But Elijah brings them back to the reality of what they were before God, by setting these twelve stones before them in the midst. Then the bullock is put upon the altar. He calls upon His God. The fire comes from heaven, consuming the sacrifice. The people are dismayed, Baal's prophets are abashed, and Elijah sees to it on the spot that the false prophets are slain and that the name of God is upheld in all its honor and dignity before his own people. It is a reminder to us all that God's name is inexorably linked with the fire of judgment and the bullock of sacrifice. It turns our eyes to the Cross of Calvary, reminding us that any religion that does not include the Cross of Calvary is idolatry.

The civilized world is full of false cults today, and all of them have this one thing in common—that they deny the efficacy of the blood of Christ. They deny the work of the Cross as the only atonement for men in their sins, and they ride in pride upon the idolatry of their own opinion that man can get back to God apart from the death and resurrection of Christ. How needful that we should remind ourselves that "as Moses lifted up the serpent in the wilderness, even so the Son of man must be lifted up that whosoever believeth in Him should not perish, but have everlasting life"!

God is holy and the fire of judgment a divine necessity to punish sin. Idolatry will present many substitutes for the work of the Cross, but there is no fire—no judgment—in these schemes. Only in the Cross of our Lord Jesus is sin dealt with in judgment. He bore our judgment there; the fire of God's wrath fell upon His Holy Head, that we might go free and be saved eternally.

Chapter VI

ELIJAH'S TRIUMPHANT FAITH

We are retracing the colorful career of that remarkable man of the Old Testament, Elijah, the Prophet. His story is told to us graphically enough in the 17th and 18th chapters of the 1st Book of Kings. It is by no means ancient history in the antiquated sense, for the anecdote might be a leaf taken from the book of the lives of one in the present modern and sophisticated age of the twentieth century.

His varied career is one of lights and shadows, ups and downs. In experiences that are familiarly parallel to our own, his pathway is most undulating. First we see him on the heights of triumphant testimony for his God as he presents an embattled bulwark against the inroads of wickedness and idolatry in the city. Then we see him in the deep shadows of retirement and loneliness encamped by the propitious shores of a meandering brook on the lonely desert. His retirement is still more picturesque as he makes his further descent into Gentile country to subsist in company with a destitute widow and her son, upon the cruse of oil that fails not, and the barrel of meal that does not waste. Then the course of his life takes a sudden upswing once more and brings him out of the shadows of retirement into the full light of testimony again.

In this new life he stands majestic and with great elegance as he rebukes the unworthy Obadiah, whose spineless expediencey is reproved in the presence of the courage and staunch faith of this man of God. Then Ahab, the King, whose wickedness outmatched all his predecessors, finds himself equally abashed before the uncompromising grandeur of Elijah's testimony. Thus we have traveled with him from the heights of his witness in the wicked city down into the valley of his loneliness with his God by the brook, across the plains of his isolation to the Gentile city to come up again and stand on the sunny slopes of Mt. Carmel to watch this man of God shine in his true color of courageous testimony.

The prophets of Baal had been put to shame when the vast multitude of all Israel had gathered together on that mountainside in giant carnival setting to watch Elijah's triumph over their false gods. These iniquitous and false prophets had built an altar, placed their bullock upon it; had whined their empty petitions throughout long hours of unavailing devotions until they were crestfallen and exposed for what they truly were, false prophets.

A DRAMATIC SPECTACLE

Now Elijah stepped forth to give the grand performance. His act was the grand finale of this impelling drama. Nor was the man of God without an eye to supreme dramatic effect which we easily discern from his masterly stage setting. The rubbish and debris of Baal's broken altar was cleared from the stage. Twelve stones, one for every tribe in Israel, were mounted in the center of the great amphitheatre as thousands of anxious eyes watched the spectacle. Then Elijah with confident skill—that confidence that had been begotten by faith in the living God whom he had learned to trust by the lonely brook as well as in the attic of the Gentile widow's home—with that same assurance of faith, he carefully laid the altar of stone.

I delight to watch him there, in his humble but confident dignity, as he builds the altar around the stones, laying every log with that precision with which a master builder constructs a foundation for a cathedral. Log upon log it rises until the stones are hidden within its compass. Then the live bullock is taken and the man of God, Elijah, who could handle sword and spear and knife with the same dexterous skill with which he could build an altar, slays the bullock, divides him in his pieces, and ranges the flesh upon the wood. There is nothing hurried about his operation. He knows that he is setting the stage for the grand climax in a victorious pageant. He moves unhurriedly, with neither haste nor wasted effort. When the animal is dressed, flayed and laid in order upon the wood, he is satisfied that everything is ready for the fire which he confidently expects to come down from heaven.

But no! He is not ready! Now he takes a spade, digs a trench, four square, around the altar. It is as broad as a double furrow. It runs all around the altar so no one can come near to touch that sacrifice without crossing that deep ditch. Then we watch the man of God once more as he turns to those around him who have now had courage enough, since they have see the discomfiture of the ungodly enemy, to come forth and take their place a little nearer to Elijah, the man of God. He calls upon them to bring four barrels of water. Whatever might he have in mind with these? But it is soon evident. As they are hurriedly brought to him, he orders that the barrels be held high upon their shoulders and the water poured directly over the whole sacrifice. The water drenches the slain animal and all over the logs it goes. Down from the altar it flows until the surplus is caught in the trench which the prophet has dug around the altar. But this is not enough! To make doubly sure that he will not be accused of any kind of fakery in perhaps conveying concealed fire to consume the sacrifice, he calls for another four barrels of water, and again the whole thing is drenched from top to bottom.

THE FIRE FALLS

In his performance this man of God will ask no quarter. If any odds have to be given they will be given in favor of his enemies. By his own special invitation, the idolatrous prophets of Baal have been brought there, four hundred and fifty strong, whilst he, a lone figure, stands as the ambassador for Jehovah. As though to add further ignominy to their certain defeat, Elijah is going to demonstrate to them that he will make the task of his own performance as difficult as he possibly can. No one is ever going to accuse this man of God that he has allowed a spark to remain hidden among the logs that he laid with such care. That is why he has drenched the altar and all that is upon it twice over. No, it was not twice over! He has it done a third time, the four barrels are refilled and water again splashed lavishly over the altar so that everyone would be thoroughly convinced that any stray spark that might have gotten in among the wood was sure to be put out by three drenchings. Now he stands back.

A great hush of silence falls upon the multitude as they watch. But Elijah lingers still. Evidently he is waiting for something. The multitude must have wondered at the delay, and I can imagine some misgiving creeping into the hearts of those seven thousand secret believers who trembled with honest doubts. But Elijah is waiting for something very definite. He turns towards the western sky, now aglow in sunset splendor. The sun's fiery disc lies low on the horizon. It is not quite set. This master performance is going to take place precisely at *sunset*. Why? Because this was the hour of Israel's sacrifice, the hour that Jehovah had decreed that the evening oblation should be made. The prophet waits in silence and, as the sun's rim dips below the horizon, the stentorian voice of Elijah is heard across the hushed landscape. "Lord God of Abraham, Isaac and of Israel"—what? No Jacob in his prayer! No, it is Israel, "a prince with God!" "Let it be known this day that thou art God in Israel and that I am thy servant, and that I have done all these things *at thy Word.* Hear me, Oh Lord, hear me, that this people may know that *thou art the Lord God* and that thou hast turned their hearts back again."

As the words of the petition of the prophet died in echo in the adjoining hills, a deeper silence ensued. Then suddenly, with lightning stroke, and thunder crash, a flash of fire rent the twilight shadows and fell square upon Elijah's altar. It consumed the sacrifice and the wood, and even the stones and the dust went up in flame, licking up the water that was in the trench. The thousands gathered upon the hillside looked on aghast with wonder as only smoldering ashes remained. Never had lightning flash fallen like this. It was God's answer to all man's doubts! At once it turned the hearts of God's people back to Himself and left the false prophets defeated and ashamed. Soon these iniquitous idolators were slain and the Name of Jehovah was glorified.

A HUMBLE MAN

Now let us notice Elijah's behaviour. Never had he shone more brilliantly as a witness for God. His spectacular feat had outmatched the very fondest expectations of the people. Surely they would put him upon a pinnacle now! They would turn their backs upon Ahab, the wicked King, and his more wicked queen, Jezebel. Now Elijah would be their man, to lead them in triumph everywhere. He would be decked with garlands and crowned with glory. Any of us who know our hearts at all well, know that, if we had been in Elijah's shoes, we would have lingered at the scene to bask in the sunlight of our own glory, to listen to the acclamations of our fellows. But Elijah sought no personal honor. He was a man of God!

The record in 1st Kings 18 then gives us a sudden change of scene. Instead of basking in the light of his new-won fame, Elijah turns to the wicked Ahab, the faithless monarch under whose protection idolatry had flourished in the land. He says: "Get thee up, eat and drink, for there is a sound of an abundance of rain." The people were now recovered for God and the rain would come. Elijah already heard the sound of it although the ears of the people were not yet tuned to the melody of the raindrops. Then Elijah slipped quietly away from the multitude. He sought no exaltation. On the other hand, he retired over the shoulder of the mountainside and the next view we have of him is that he is alone with His God, and the record tells us, "he cast himself down on the earth and put his face between his knees." Oh, how unlike the behaviour of the man of the world is that of the man of faith! When he has to witness for His God in public, he will stand upright, his head held high in the elevation of his calling; he will present himself in the majesty of the Name of the Lord whom he serves, but, having witnessed a good confession in behalf of His God, and knowing the frailty of his flesh, he will bow low in reverence and in gratitude, his head between his knees.

One cannot read of all this without being impressed with the example which is set forth for every Christian man and woman. It is only he who can humble himself before His God in the attitude of abject dependence, who can really triumph on the field of conquest. It is he who can lean hard upon Jehovah after a fight is won that will stand most upright in the day of conflict. I find the truth of this great story re-echoed in the New Testament where Paul, the great Apostle, says in Phil. 3:3: "For we are the circumcision which worship God in the spirit and rejoice in Christ Jesus and have no confidence in the flesh." That is the true Christian attitude. Courage in the day of battle; staunchness in his testimony, yet willing at the first opportunity to retire in communion with his God, bowed upon his knees and his head touching the dust—"no confidence in the flesh."

Prostrate before His God, Elijah remains in earnest prayer. Without raising his head, he calls his servant, bids him take the trail to the hilltop where he may scan the entire canopy of heaven for sign of rain. It must have seemed a long time before the servant returned to find Elijah still upon his knees, his head bent low, to tell him the stars shone bright in a cloudless sky. "Go a second time," and, as he went, Elijah prayed for rain. Surely God would not fail him, but it was the waiting that tried the prophet. Then the servant returned a second time—still no sign of rain. Again he took the trail up over the hill at his master's bidding. It seemed a useless trek. Again and again through the long night hours the servant hiked the mountain slope always to bring the disappointing and monotonous words—"no change."

Yet still Elijah prayed. And every praying heart knows the suspense of such prayer.

Six times his servant took the lonely trail; six times he returned with the report — weather clear; sky cloudless; no change! "Go again," said the prophet. What? A seventh time? "What a useless waste of time!" said the fleshly mind. "Go!" said faith. Then, as the servant scanned with weary eyes the whole canopy of heaven once more—there, off yonder in the eastern sky out over the Mediterranean, — it was but a shadow of dimness. He must have rubbed his eyes and looked again. Yes! it was a cloud, but so small you could hardly consider it; so far away, so insignificant, just the size of a man's hand. But he hastens back to Elijah and announces the scanty evidence. That is it!—says Elijah. Seven times the servant had gone while Elijah prayed. Now the answer! Why seven?

Seven in Scripture is ever the complete and perfect number. James in the New Testament tells us: "The trying of your faith worketh patience; but let patience have her perfect work, that ye may be perfect and entire, wanting nothing." It was seven times the leper dipped in Jordan—now faith waits seven times on God. Our prayer must have the same earnestness with which we first came as sinners to be forgiven. Jehovah wanted to teach Elijah that patient waiting upon God, even to the limit of endurance—seven times—would bring the answer.

Let that number "seven" in Elijah's prayer life be for your encouragement always. Even then the evidence was so very little; only a little cloud the size of a man's hand; and what was that in so great an expanse of sky! But Elijah believed it was the forerunner of abundant blessing and he waited upon Jehovah. Don't let us ever give up! Soon the cloud increased in size and gradually the whole canopy of the heavens became overcast until a thunderous pall of blackness shut out the stars. Then came the wind and the raindrops began to fall. Elijah rises from his knees as the raindrops splash his gladdened countenance. Three and a half years' drought is broken and the thirsty earth drinks in the rain that now falls in torrents. "The effectual fervent prayer of a righteous man availeth much." Thus we are reminded that the Christian pathway has its highlights of brilliant testimony, but it has its deep shadows of waiting upon God. You cannot have the one without the other. "They that wait upon the Lord shall renew their strength, they shall mount up with wings as eagles, they shall run and not be weary, they shall walk and not faint."

Chapter VII

ELIJAH UNDER THE JUNIPER TREE

In following Elijah's career there is one outstanding characteristic that strikes us forcibly. It is its undulating and changeful character. I wonder if this is not the reason why his story appeals so much to our hearts. Like that of Elijah, the Christian's life today is one of great contrasts. Our pathway lies across a country of towering mountain peaks and dark valleys; through sunshine and shadow. Often we feel we must walk across rough and trackless desert, then again we come out upon the smooth highway of the high plateau of Christian experience. Sometimes we bask in the sunshine of God's goodness; then again our journey lies across the unprotected tableland where storm and hurricane beat against us. Perhaps that is the main reason why God has put into this wonderful book of the Old Testament the story of the undulating experiences of Elijah, the Prophet, that we all might read of it and take heart and press onward.

Thus we follow the fluctuating curve of circumstance that makes up this man's life. First, a man of prayer and then a champion of righteousness in public testimony in a wicked city; then down yonder by the lonely brook, thence into the forgotten region of the Gentile country to subsist upon the scant sustenance of the poor widow with the barrel of meal that wasted not and the cruse of oil that did not fail. Then we see this man rise out of the isolation of his retirement to come forth in the majesty of his faith, to denounce the wicked Ahab, king of Israel, who had departed from God; to put to shame the faithless Obadiah, whose cowardly and spineless conduct belied the faith that smoldered so feebly in his heart. Then we watch Elijah go with the Israel hosts to the sunny slopes of Mt. Carmel, there to bring to a climax the controversy which existed between the people of Israel and their God. We note the brilliant achievement of the man of God when he put to utter discomfiture all the idolatrous wickedness of the followers of Baal. We see him rise in the glory of his triumph as the fire from heaven came down and consumed the sacrifice upon the altar which he had built with his own hands. Flushed with his victory, he had slain the four hundred and fifty false prophets and then retired to the shoulder of the hill to bow his worthy head to the dust, waiting upon God to send the rain.

We see him rise from his knees, lifting his grateful countenance to the heavens above as the rain descends in torrents upon the parched land of Israel. His triumph seemed to be so supreme that we are apt to think that now nothing could happen to discourage this man. He has brought his people back to God, he has put the enemy to flight, and I can see him then, his face wreathed in the smile of complacent triumph, standing in the teeming rain, his cloak gathered about him. Then he starts down the hill and comes upon Ahab, the wicked King, seated in the royal chariot there by the side of the mountain road, high on Carmel's heights. The royal equipage must have been a dejected and bedraggled spectacle, chariot and horses drenched in the rain, its multicolored and ornamental plumage hanging limp, the king and all his courtiers enjoying the unexpected rain bath that had so suddenly come upon them. We envision Elijah as he stands there with that complacent air of having gained the day. It was his hour!

There had been a time when Elijah had to seek eclipse for himself in retirement, when he had to turn his back upon Ahab and all his wicked followers, and seek isolation by the brookside out on the desert. But now he had come into his own. It had been demonstrated to all that he was Jehovah's servant, and it is he who now dictates to Ahab, the King. He tells Ahab, if he ever hopes to get back to the city, he had better make haste. Soon the mountain road would be impassable and the heavy royal chariot would be bogged down in the mud. So he enjoins the king with all his company to proceed at once, and I can see them go off in the drenching rain, the gallant horses at a full gallop, the mud flying from the chariot wheels.

It was certainly a triumphant hour for everyone, but especially for Elijah, and the record goes on to tell us that, in spite of all the speed of the horses, Elijah actually reached the city before they did. Evidently the Spirit of God came upon Elijah and carried him by supernatural and divine power, down the mountain side and across the plains with even greater switness than the charging steeds of the royal chariots. When the king and his royal equipage came dashing toward the city of Jezreel, there stood Elijah calm and majestic beside the city gate awaiting their arrival. It was an hour of great triumph for Elijah.

Then for several days it would seem as though Elijah slipped from sight. During that time, Ahab, whose evil heart was still unchanged, re-established himself at the palace, and in the good graces of his wicked wife Queen Jezebel. No doubt he related in great detail the triumphs which Elijah had gained on the mountain top of Carmel; how the wicked prophets of Baal had been slain to the last man. The anger of Jezebel rose to iniquitous heights, and she sent a message at once to Elijah, the prophet. Just as surely as her favored prophets had been slain so she will seek his life.

Then in the 19th chapter of 1st Kings, a most astonishing change of events takes place in the life of Elijah. We see the man who had stood so recently on Mt. Carmel, in all the elegance of his triumph in witness for the Lord, suddenly being seized with an unexplained terror. He who had stood with such valor before four hundred and fifty men, flees in fear from the face of a woman. Off he goes, taking only his servant with him, out across the rain-soaked plains as far from the city as his trembling legs will carry him, wishing only to be as far removed as possible from the fearsome countenance of the wicked Jezebel. We do not wonder altogether at his terror, for, after all, in the sacred record of the Scripture, this woman's name has become synonymous with apostate religion. She appears symbolically in the book of Revelation as the all-powerful patron of idolatrous religion without God, and her voice, even in this day and age, has been heard and has spoken fear to many a humble servant of Christ. Those who seek to preach the truth of God solely in dependence upon Him without giving an answer to organized religious authority know something of its terror.

Now we follow the faltering footsteps of the crestfallen Elijah as he finds his lonely way across the desert, the sweet odor of earth's refreshment from the recent rains still filling the atmosphere, and the sun, now high in the heavens, beating upon his head. A full day's journey he goes. For twenty-four hours he trudges aimlessly onward, caring little for the direction as long as it took him further and further away from the habitation of the wicked queen. Then, tired and way-worn, he comes upon a juniper tree. The dark shade of its branches seem to match the shadowy dullness of his own spirit. So he sits down in the deepest despondency by its gnarled trunk. Crestfallen, beaten, and well-nigh heartbroken, there he sits long and lingeringly in the depths of misery and despair. Without lifting his weary eyes to heaven, now screened by the overhanging branches, he cries out to God: "It is enough, now, oh Lord, take away my life for I am not better than my fathers."

Elijah's plea wakes an echo in many a Christian heart! "It is enough!" You look back over your shoulder, like Elijah, and you think of your devotion to the Lord; you think of the way in which you have served your friends, and it has been so ill-requited. Like Elijah, there have been occasions when you thought you had reached the pinnacle of success in your Christian service. There was a sense of triumph in your soul.

You have seen men affected by your witness for Christ; you have seen hearts turned to God by what you have said; and it gave you that kindly glow of self-satisfaction, radiating throughout your whole being, and you felt so content with yourself and your service. Then some head was raised, an enemy upon whom you did not calculate! Perhaps an unkindly critic—maybe a jealous fellow-worker—maybe the official hand of the board of elders of the organized church or meeting to which you belong. To you it was like a Jezebel that threatened your very life, and so you wandered out into the wilderness of disappointment, out of the sunshine and warmth of the kindly love of God. Like Elijah under the juniper tree, you sat down in the shadows, wrapped your great cloak about you in self-pity and said: "It is enough!" Then, as you reflected upon your own career, those deficiencies and failures that had seemed so unimportant and insignificant in the light of your triumphs, began to loom so big and so humiliating in your eyes. Then perhaps you said like Elijah: "Oh, Lord, take away my life, for I am no better than my fathers." Your sense of failure was overwhelming. Indeed your estimate of yourself "under the juniper tree" would beggar description.

TAKE COURAGE

Let us take a good look at what God did for Elijah. It is recorded so beautifully for us in 1st Kings, chapter 19. First, God put him to sleep. His servant needed a rest and, as he slept, an angel touched him. This would have its counterpart in this Christian age in the ministry of the Holy Spirit Himself, whose divine comfort is poured into our souls, yes, even sometimes when we are asleep. As Elijah slept soundly under the juniper tree, the angel said to him: "Rise up and eat. And he looked, and behold, a cake, baken on the coals and a cruse of water, and he ate and drank and laid him down again." Then the angel roused him again and Elijah evidently sat down to a regular banquet, and he ate and drank so much that he went on the strength of that banquet for forty days and forty nights without getting hungry.

What a magnificent picture of the comforting and reviving power of the ministry of our God! The world loves to see us discouraged; the devil mocks at us when we sit down under "the juniper tree," but God draws near, pillows our head upon His own endless love, underneath us He puts His own everlasting arms. We rest sweetly in all our weakness upon His fathomless affection and His endless power; He revives us with His own sustaining grace. How like the Psalmist's words! "Me maketh me to lie down in green pastures, He restoreth my soul; thou preparest a table before me in the presence of mine enemies, thou anoinest my head with oil, my cup runneth over." (Psalm 23:4.)

May the Lord ever encourage us to feel that we are just as much in the hollow of the Lord's own hand when we are in the valley of despondenecy as we are on the mountain top of testimony! Surely the Christian life is one of undulating vicissitudes; now on the heights, then in the valley, now in the sunshine, then in the shade, but wherever it may be, it is worth while, for we are ever learning the lesson of the endless, unchangeable and unfathomable love of our Lord and Saviour.

Chapter VIII

ELIJAH — THE STILL SMALL VOICE

We have been observing again and again that the spiritual fortunes of this illustrious man of God, Elijah of the Old Testament, were most fluctuating in character. Like most of us he seems to have been a man of spiritual extremes, now on the mountaintop of spiritual vigor and superabundant energy of faith, then again taking the low road down in the valley of Christian experience.

We have contemplated the prophet in abject despondency under the shade of the juniper tree, a day's journey from the city, away out on the desert, occupied in that most miserable of all idle pursuits—self-occupation. Elijah really hit bottom in his spiritual experience in spite of the fact that he had been so recently on the hilltop of triumphant testimony. Nevertheless, just as God had stood by him on Mount Carmel when he had so dramatically enacted a scene of defiance against the false prophets of Baal, even so now God was with him. As he lay asleep under the juniper tree, it was the everlasting arms of Jehovah that upheld him, it was the hand of His Lord that provided a banquet whereof he partook enough to sustain him for forty days and forty nights thereafter.

THE HERMIT

One would very well imagine that when Elijah would rouse himself from so strange a slumber that he would at once be restored to his former vigor of faith. In this we are mistaken. His conduct exemplifies the inconsistencies of our own human frailty, for, when he stands upon his feet, instead of returning at once to the city to speak defiance before the wicked Jezebel in the name of Jehovah, he decides rather to flee still farther. Methinks he wants to run away from himself now. He sets out across the wilderness until his dejected eyes fall upon Mount Horeb in the distance. Along the mountainside he comes until he finds a cave. He goes into its deepest recesses. He feels that this is the kind of place for a man like him. However well the Lord may have treated him by His heavenly kindness, he cannot forget how badly he has been treated by his brethren and by the world. The most remote isolation is what he wants now. Thus he becomes a lonely cave-dweller on a barren mountainside.

However honored Elijah may have been in his life of testimony in days so recently passed, it would seem now that his life of retirement is a rare and picturesque illustration of the life of the Christian who has become wearied in well-doing, whose footsteps lag and falter on the heavenly climb of faith's difficult pathway. It is truly a danger that confronts us all. It is a sad fact that so many of us are either asleep under the juniper tree or hidden in the cave of our own enforced isolation. Many Christians can look back to a time in their lives, I am sure, when they climbed the hill of Christian experience with steady steps and unfaltering determination. The light of their testimony, although perhaps not so brilliant as that of Elijah on Mt. Carmel, yet shone with starlight lustre in the darkness of the world. With agile willingness they ran the errands of mercy and kindness at the behest of their Lord and Master. Readily enough they seized the opportunity of speaking a word in season to him that was weary. The joy bells of love's first carols chimed in their soul so that the melody of their happy testimony for Christ was heard across this world's bleak landscape. Now it is changed!

There came a time in your life perhaps when you felt like Elijah, that in spite of your sense of triumph before God, you were misunderstood, misjudged, unappreciated. In those very regions where friends should have been generous in your praise, some wicked Jezebel threatened your life. Instead of being hailed by your brethren for the brilliance of your testimony, they were apathetic and unresponsive and viewed you with a kind of tolerance that sapped the vital goodness of your zeal. Although you unsheathed your sword readily enough against the world's false prophets, your brethren thought you were only seeking self-prominence. Jealousy's green eye followed you everywhere. Your spiritual life was threatened and you fled the scene. Gradually the spiritual slumber of despondency laid you low in the deep shadows of the juniper branches, or you went further out in the wilderness like Elijah, and sought complete eclipse for your light of testimony in a hermit's cave.

THE DEFEATIST'S CAVE

Oh, how true it is of so many of us! Many are either slumbering under the juniper tree of self-occupation, or hiding in the cave of defeatism on the barren mountainside far out in the wilderness. This is partially true in the hearts and lives of most of us who call ourselves Christians in these difficult days, and there are good arguments in favor of our retirement. It should lift our spirits then to see how God dealt further with Elijah when he became a cave-dweller.

It is recorded for us in 1st Kings, chapter 19, that the Lord came to his rocky dwelling and He says to him—mark it *well*!—"What doest thou here, Elijah?" Methinks this was the grandest kind of reproof! His "self-occupation" under the juniper tree had led directly to his "no-occupation" in Horeb's rugged cave. "What doest thou here, Elijah?" Oh that the echo of this might resound through the deepest recesses of our souls today! "What doest thou here?" He who had so recently stood courageously forth in the sunshine of Carmel's mount, now lurks idly in the deep shadows of the mountain cave, a spiritual hermit. Is it not most expressive of the doldrums of apathy and defeatism into which so many of us who are Christians have drifted? Once so active for the Lord, the devil's opiates of self-pity and self-occupation have robbed us of our zeal. "What doest thou here, Elijah?"

Then the prophet gives forth a most pitiable lament concerning his own goodness and the failures of others. "*I* have been very jealous," he says, "for the Lord God of Hosts, *but* the children of Israel have forsaken thy covenant and I, even I only, am left." Are there not countless genuine Christian hearts cast by the wayside of life in this same atttiude? You have left the church to which you once went with such godly zeal because the devil persuaded you that there were so many unreal people in that church and you were so real yourself. We have all gone that road at times. Many Christians seemed so inconsistent! Their lives corresponded so little to their profession that we decided to leave them all behind and we trudged off across the desert of separation until we came to our Mt. Horeb, crept into a dark spiritual cave to dwell in our own lonely habitation. If that is your story or mine, let us take a look then at what God demonstrated to Elijah in such spectacular fashion as He speaks with him there within the darkness of that cave.

Let us in fancy sit now on the rocky ledge beside the dispirited Prophet as he gazes through the shadows out into the sunlight. It is as though we sat together with Elijah in a great amphitheatre, high in the gallery, looking down on the panorama beneath where Jehovah Himself is about to enact a supreme drama of elemental forces of all nature's grandeur. First comes *a violent wind.* It is of hurricane force. We first hear it sigh in the distant hills across the desert. It comes across the valley like the noise of a rushing torrent or a thundering herd of a thousand hoofs. Then, as we watch from our vantage point, we see it as a mighty tornado, dust-laden and black, tearing across the open plateau and down through the valley, uprooting trees, leveling everything before it as though the Almighty Himself had taken a giant switch-broom and swept the valley clean in mighty power from end to end. Then, as we hear the rushing noise die away in the hills beyond, a great hush falls upon the landscape and we hear the word of the Lord: "God is not in *the whirlwind.*"

But the drama is not over, and we sit spellbound watching for the next act. Soon it comes. The noise of the wind was as nothing to this. The whole earth trembles. A *great earthquake* seems to rock all creation to its very foundation and we sit terrified at the ominous impact of the mighty temblor. The hills reel and totter in thunderous clatter before our bewildered vision. It is soon over. As the rocking earth seems again to settle beneath us, Elijah looks out once more, and realizes that God is not in *the earthquake.*

But there is a third act much more spectacular than the former two. It is *fire* now. From our seat above the valley, we see the mighty entrancing display. It is thunder, lightning, wild fire and Aurora Borealis all rolled into one, as though God Himself had unleashed the very source of lightning as a fiery chariot that dashes across the dome of heaven with ear-splitting violence, setting everything aflame in dazzling brightness and blinding sheen. But God is not in *the fire.* And silence again falls upon the stage.

Then the final act. This is neither whirlwind, nor earthquake, nor fire, but out of the stillness of the shadows there is heard *a still, small voice.* What an anticlimax to the spectacular pageant we have just seen! It is most unimpressive after the fiery display, the rumbling earthquake, and the howling wind. But, however feeble it may be, *God was in it.* It was His voice!

Now from our seat on the rocky ledge we take a look at Elijah, the Prophet. There is a subdued quietness in his eyes that was not there before, for God has taught him a great lesson, namely, that Jehovah has many servants, but it is the least of them all, the most insignificant, the quietest that He uses most. The humblest man who has renounced himself is His best servant. The Lord was reminding Elijah that He needed not the spectacular, the loud thundering trumpet blast. The still small voice, if God is in it, will reach men's hearts. "For God hath chosen the weak things of the world to confound the mighty, the base things of the world, and things that are despised, hath God chosen, yea, and things which are not, to bring to naught things that are, that no flesh should glory in His presence." (1 Cor. 1:27-28.)

ASHAMED YET ENCOURAGED

When Elijah learns this lesson, he stands up, wraps his mantle about him and steps forth from the cave. Then God graciously discloses to him, that, although he may be but a *still small voice* in the land of Israel, yet he has big things for him to do. He commissions him to appoint a new king over Syria and one to succeed King Ahab in Israel, and to appoint a successor for himself in Elisha, the prophet, because the Lord is going to take him up in a fiery chariot to a heavenly world. Meantime he whispers in his ear a gentle reminder that he still has seven thousand other servants in Israel that have not bowed the knee in idolatry. Surely Elijah was both a little ashamed and greatly encouraged. May the Lord do likewise for each one of us as we reflect upon this great incident in Elijah's varied career.

Chapter IX

ELIJAH — ON THE HILLTOP

There is one keynote to Elijah's interesting life of service—it is "separation from the world." Unlike many of these illustrious patriarchs of Old Testament Scripture, whose interests were intimately entwined with the national, social, and spiritual lives of their people, Elijah traverses the stage in an aloofness of sanctity that is truly arresting. Like a crescent moon on a winter's long-lived night passing low across the world's horizon, now flooding the landscape with its silvery light, then darting into obscurity behind the lowering clouds to appear again as unexpectedly, so Elijah travels across one of the darkest nights of Israel's history. He is uniquely the heavenly man whose testimony shines with fitful and changing light as he comes out brilliantly at times, to retire once more to the obscurity and aloofness of his heavenly character.

In 1 Kings, chapter 19, Elijah steps forth from the shadows of the cave, and there opens up before him a new and enlarged vista of service upon which he immediately sets forth with reverence and fear. Leaving the dreary waste of Horeb behind, for Horeb means "desert," let us again set off across the plains with Elijah, who now travels with a new vigor. A new light shines in his eye, because a new hope has been born in his spirit. The Lord has disclosed that, although he may seem weak and paltry among his apathetic and idolatrous people, yet God has a grander and a better world in which he will shine with undimmed brilliance, and to which he is about to be translated. Instead of abandoning the scene of his triumphs and failures here on earth in the despondency of his own self-pity, begging the Lord to take away his life, he is going to make a grand, triumphal exit in a chariot of fire. He will leave behind him the foreign and disappointing elements of unbelief in his nation, to travel in power and majesty across the blue of heaven in dazzling splendour to his own native sphere in that land above the sun.

HE FINDS ELISHA

Before Elijah makes his departure heavenward, there remains some unfinished business on the earth. It is urgent business, and there is no time to waste, hence the quickened footsteps of the prophet as he journeys back across the desert. Soon the fertile and undulating hills come into view, and we travel with him, in fancy, straight as an arrow across the fields, for he has a tryst to keep with a man called Elisha, who is to be left in charge after he himself has made the grand ascent. It is springtime, as it is always springtime for those who expect translation, a glad reminder of the blessed hope within the hearts of all Christians even in this dark hour. The budding trees and fresh verdure speak of better things to come as we journey on. Presently we come to a large field of upturned sod. Twelve skillful ploughmen guide their plough-shares across the rich bosom of the good earth. Like Samuel looking over the sons of Jesse, Elijah lets them all go by until the last, the least significant, pulls abreast with his yolk of oxen and his plough. With that deliberation and purpose which ever accompanies the assurance of faith, Elijah walks over to this twelfth ploughman, divests himself of the mantle that hung about his own shoulders, and places it upon the shoulders of the country lad whose name was Elisha. It is a simple, God-given token that this young man would be Elijah's successor as the prophet of Israel. As God always does, so does Elijah on this occasion, he chooses the last ploughman, for it is ever in the economy of God's magnificent grace that the last shall be first and the first last.

THE KING MUST DIE

One link of duty that had bound Elijah to the earth beneath has now been severed. The yolk of his service has been duly laid upon his worthy successor and he is now free to make his grand departure. As he does on so many other occasions, Elijah now seems to slip from the record to make way for the story of God's dealings with His rebellious people, but he reappears in the unique and solitary majesty of his aloof and heavenly testimony, in the first chapter of the next book, the Second Book of Kings.

He comes with picturesque suddenness upon the scene again. The wicked king Ahab has received the merited fate of his ungodliness, as has his still more wicked queen Jezebel. Their unworthy stars have sunk in the murky waters of judgment and there now sits upon the throne of Israel, Ahab's son, Ahaziah, who followed in his father's wicked foodsteps. He had evidently been parading himself on the roof garden of his palace, had stumbled and fallen through the lattice work, and lay injured and sick upon his bed. In his sickness he sent messengers to beseech the help of a false god and Elijah reappears suddenly in the way to confront his messengers.

Evidently Elijah had been long since forgotten, for they do not recognize him. But, with the unique authority of a man with a heavenly message, he tells them to return to their master with the sad news that he will never rise from his bed of sickness, but he will die. It is the startling requital for his idolatrous wickedness. Heaven's throne has been violated, for he who sat upon the throne of David had turned his back upon the Lord of Hosts and had sought temporal help from the hand of a false god. It is a national disgrace and Elijah recognizes it in the death sentence which he pronounces on the king. The messengers return posthaste to their royal master who questions them concerning this strange personage who appeared to them in the way. They describe him. He is a hairy man and girt about with a leathern girdle. The king says—*"It is Elijah."*

Thus God's servants are ever marked. They are not hard to recognize. Their venerable appearance may be the subject of the mockery of unbelievers when the weather is fair, but thy are sought out diligently in the day of adversity. Elijah's hairy appearance and his girdle of leather may seem antiquated and unadorned in the world's eye, yet they bespeak the simplicity of his heart and the separation of his walk from a world gone mad with idolatrous pleasure.

ON TOP OF A HILL

Having ascertained that it is really Elijah, the king sends forth a company of soldiers, fifty in number, and a captain in charge. They go out from the city and the Scripture says very graphically: "They went up to him; behold he sat on the top of a hill." How picturesquely unique this is! I wonder if it is a reminder to us all, that the true servant of God is ever in that same exalted eminence above the scheming and complex affairs of men. In New Testament language we are reminded of the present position of the people of God. They are truly on top of a hill. The Ephesian Epistle tells us that "we are risen with Christ, and made to sit together in heavenly places in Christ Jesus, that in the ages to come He might show the exceeding riches of His grace in His kindness toward us through Christ Jesus." How jealous the Christian should be of his heavenly calling, of his heavenly position, his hill-top character, even as he journeys like Elijah through a world gone mad with God-forgetfulness, where the darkness of unbelief and hatred envelop the scene! So we find Elijah sitting in grand isolation on top of a hill. The tragic story of what follows is truly arresting.

THEY BOW THE KNEE

The captain of fifty approaches with boldness and commands Elijah to come down and go to his royal master, but military might means nothing to this man of faith. Elijah calls down fire from heaven that consumes the whole company of soldiers, including their leader. When news of this reaches the king, another fifty with their captain are sent out with the same command and with the same results. The fire of judgment consumes them. Again the king calls another fifty soldiers. A wiser captain is put in charge and they journey out, and up the hillside to confront Elijah. There he sits in the solitary dignity of his heavenly position. He is staunch and uncompromising. As far as he is concerned now, the whole world lies in the wicked one and he himself has his eyes upward waiting for his translation to a better and a grander world.

The third captain of fifty makes a different approach to Elijah. I can see the fifty soldiers with their ranking officer out yonder on the hillside. Elijah sits there hairy and gaunt in his simple attire, unmoved in his dignified solitude. They get down on their knees before him. They realize that they are in the presence of God's representative, a heavenly man, and their hearts are contrite. They bow low before him. Instead of a command, a prayer comes from their lips, and grace instead of judgment descends upon their heads. Their lives are spared. Yet the punishment of the wicked king who had desecrated his royal and holy office must be carried out and they have to return to their royal master with a repeated death sentence.

ON GOD'S RIGHT HAND

One cannot leave this scene without noticing so forcefully that Elijah is here a magnificent type of our Lord in inexorable righteousness, willing to give grace to the humble. He is *high upon a hill,* for He is on the right hand of the majesty on high? Since

His rejection by the world, He sits there in the dignity of perfect holiness. The world was given its opportunitly of unmerited favor when Jesus the Lord journeyed across this world in kindly grace. Now He has been cast out, but God has raised Him from among the dead, seated Him at His own right hand, and made Him a Prince and a Saviour. To those who come on bended knee like these soldiers to Elijah, laying down the weapons of their own efforts, He speaks in kindly grace. For the proud unbeliever who stands in the marshalled strength of his own self-righteousness and refuses to bow at His feet, He has nothing but judgment.

How I would urge that this simple story of Elijah might carry home to our hearts the message of God's uncompromising attitudes towards our sins, and His unmerited grace to the sinner who confesses his sins! He has declared the whole world guilty before Him, and He has set forth Christ as the only Saviour. His mandate is that he who will bow the knee and confess Him as Lord will be saved. But he who refuses will be condemned. Even as we read in John, chapter three—"The Father loveth the Son and hath given all things into His hands. He that believeth on the Son hath everlasting life: and he that believeth *not* the Son shall not see life; but the wrath of God abideth *on him.*"

Chapter X

ELIJAH'S LAST DAY

Perhaps one of the most arresting questions that has ever been asked is this: "If you had but one day more to live in this world, what would you do with it?" The answers have been many, but we have one man's answer in the 2nd chapter of the 2nd Book of Kings. The man's name is Elijah. The Lord had disclosed to him that he was about to be translated to heaven, and he has but one day left here in this world. What shall he do with it?

Elijah was a servant of God who had spent much of his life in isolation and in waiting upon God. We have seen in retracing his footsteps how fluctuating was his career. Although it had its highlights of brilliant testimony, there was also much time spent in the shadows of obscurity, and even of eclipse so far as this world is concerned. Now this is his last day. Will he again find a juniper tree under which he may sit, awaiting the hour of his summons to another world? Or will he make a spectacular appearance before his nation in one last dramatic reproof for their idolatrous ways? He does neither. Instead he makes a tour of the countryside that he might take one last look at the four great historical shrines of the national history of his people. These four places are sacred in Israel's checkered pageant of exploits. They are: Gilgal, Bethel, Jericho and Jordan.

There is nothing of sadness about Elijah's attitude or occupation on this, the last day of his life, and the contemplation of it comes as a real challenge to everyone of us. If the span of our sojourn here on earth were shortened to a single day, I wonder what our occupation would be. Would we sit as many have done, blanched with fear and uncertainty as the words re-echoed through our souls: "It is appointed unto men once to die and after this the judgment?" Or would the lamp of faith shine brightly in our souls so that, like the Apostle Paul, we should be able to say: "For we know that if the earthly house of this tabernacle be dissolved, we have a building of God, an house not made with hands, eternal in the heavens." (2 Cor. 5:1.) With Elijah there was nothing flustered, or excited, or fearful about his movements. He knew that ere the evenings shadows fell, he would step at the Lord's bidding into the triumphal car which would take him heavenward with great glory.

GILGAL—TWELVE STONES

On his last tour of the countryside he takes along the young man whom he had appointed as his successor, Elisha, the Prophet. They start with Gilgal, thence across the plains they go to Bethel, then onward to Jericho, then to the River Jordan, across its stream dry shod, and out yonder to the wilderness whence the elder Prophet is caught up to heaven itself.

First they come to Gilgal, and what rich memories fill their hearts as they gaze upon the memorials of Israel's pageantry, recalling one of the most triumphant days in all their history! It was here that the people had made their first encampment after the miraculous crossing of Jordan. The two prophets no doubt gazed upon these memorial stones that had been taken from the bed of the river and had been set up on its banks—twelve monuments to their triumphant arrival in Canaan, in the Promised Land. There was one stone for every tribe, reminding them that, in spite of all their wanderings and their failures in their wilderness journey, God by miracle power had brought them through unscathed. It was here at Gilgal, under the providence of God, that this nation had changed overnight from a nomadic company of vagrants with tents, and moving cloud, and portable tabernacle, and constantly changing encampment, to a veritable army regimented and in martial order ready to go in to conquer and possess the land.

I can well imagine Elijah impressing upon his young friend that, in spite of all the vicissitudes of their national history from the days of Egypt's cruel bondage, onward across the Red Sea by miracle passage, then through the desert for forty years, and finally passing dry-shod through Jordan's water, that God had ever been their salvation. There had not been a moment when He had deserted them. Truly he had borne them an eagle's wings and brought them through. Gilgal was the terminus of their wanderings. Here they renewed their covenant with Jehovah, set up a memorial of twelve stones in honor of their deliverance. Surely the young Prophet would understand, as he stood among these memorials, that Elijah had brought him to Gilgal that his spirit might drink deep of the well of God's faithfulness, and that he might be strengthened for days to come.

BETHEL—ONE STONE

Having lingered over these reminiscences they must haste

onward, for is this not Elijah's last day? There is no time to waste. They travel quickly across the palm-covered acres eastward, marking the road that many pilgrim feet had trodden, for every inch of the way was sacred in Israel's memory. They come to Bethel which was in a sense the very birthplace of their national life. Here Elijah found his way to another memorial stone which meant much to them. When they found it, it was not different from a hundred others that lay about, but what memories were enshrined there! It was a rude block of unhewn rock, but upon this stone the head of the patriarch Jacob had rested on that night when, in misgiving and fear, he laid himself down on the dark plain, wondering what the morrow would bring. The stone surely made a hard pillow, but, as the patriarch lay there in fitful slumber, he dreamed of a ladder that reached up to heaven, and upon which he saw the angels ascending and descending. The scene struck such terror to his slumbering senses that he was made to cry out: "This is a terrible place, this is none other than the House of God, the very gate of heaven."

It had been this vision of a way opened up into heaven itself that had begotten in the heart of Jacob a firm faith in God's purpose. He was made to realize for a brief moment that heaven and earth were linked together in his interest. On that dark night on the plain, as he slept, Jacob cast faith's anchor into the sure promises of God, and his anchor had held, for the Lord had been faithful. It is as though Elijah was assuring his young companion that God's promises would always abide, and that, after he himself was gone to heaven, the faithfulness of Jehovah would ever be with him.

How needful it is that you and I should go back by faith with Elijah to Bethel that our spirits might be lifted up, and that we might see again that ladder that linked heaven and earth. It was a dream surely to Jacob, but a vision of the night that portrayed a great reality. Jacob saw it dimly, but you and I are in the full blaze of its light because we know that the ladder found its fulfillment in Christ Himself when He hung on Calvary's Cross. "There is one God and one mediator between God and men, the man Christ Jesus." As our Saviour and Lord was suspended between earth and heaven on Calvary's cruel Tree, He by His sacrificial work, linked heaven and earth indissolubly together, and opened up a way whereby God could reach down to man in all his misery and sin, rescue him from the pit of destruction into which he had fallen, and bring him home to Himself in courts of light.

It was where this ladder had stood, on that night when Jacob dreamed, that the history of Israel as God's people began, and it is at the Cross that our history must begin with God. Jacob called that place Bethel which means "the house of God." The Scripture tells us "whose house are we, if we hold fast the confession of our faith."

JERICHO—FAITH'S VICTORY

But we travel on with the two Prophets, for there is no time to linger. And we come back across the plains until we arrive at the city of Jericho. And what memories are awakened here! This was the city which the Israel hosts had held under siege for so long, seeking in vain some way of bringing assault upon its bastions. No power of arms that they could muster together could bring about its surrender. No military strategist had brought forth a successful plan of attack, and the armed host of the Lord had wearily encamped, crestfallen at their own impotence.

Then the Lord told them to march around this great city of Jericho. They marched seven times around the city, Joshua at their head. Then the priests, the most "unsoldierlike" men in their company, had been told to put their trumpets to their lips and blow a resounding blast. At the same time the people shouted together with a great noise and the walls of the city fell down by miracle power so that they could go in and capture it. I should like to have heard Elijah tell the story to the young Prophet Elisha, who so recently had been but a plowman, following a yolk of oxen in the field. How the young lad must have thrilled at the recounting of this valiant exploit!

Perhaps Elijah would point to one particular place in the rebuilt city, telling him that there—over yonder—had stood the house of Rahab, the harlot, the only person in all of that city who had been faithful to the Lord, and who had sheltered the spies. He would tell of the scarlet line she hung out at the window as a signal to everybody of her faith in Jehovah in spite of the fact that she was a sinner. Yes, it was a scene of great triumph, and every recollection would assure young Elisha that, even at a time when everything was black and prospects were at their worst, yet God had intervened on behalf of His people, as He always does, and they had come out in glorious victory.

How needful is this lesson for every one of us! We need to

reassure ourselves that, in spite of all the failure and shortcoming about us; in spite of the weakness and impotence that we find within our own breasts; yet the Lord is on the throne, and He is a victorious Lord on behalf of His people.

JORDAN—DEATH CONQUERED

But they move onward from Jericho, and the two Prophets come across the valley until they reach Jordan itself. As they come in sight of the muddy stream, no doubt Elijah recounted how the Lord, by miracle power, had opened up a way for the marching host through its depths. He would tell how the priests, carrying the ark of the covenant on their shoulders, had stepped into the water and how, the moment their feet had touched the stream, the waters had walled up on either side to make a dry highway across its depth and how the marching host had traveled over it. It had been a climactic day in the history of his people. Their wilderness wanderings were forever over, and Jordan's highway through the bed of the stream was their exit from the privations and anxieties of desert travel and their entrance into the Promised Land. But that was all in the past, and the question might be, was it simply an empty memory?

This same people that had traveled across Jordan in such triumph were now disunited and confused. Their monarch was an idolator, and they themselves were following strange gods. Had Jehovah then changed? Elijah gives the answer to this. From off his shoulders he takes his mantle, raises it over his head, and brings it down upon the waters of Jordan with a resounding smack. Had the Lord changed? No! The waters parted just as they had done before and they made a highway for the two wayfarers to travel across dryshod. It was not a host of thousands this time; it was only two men, but it was an eloquent testimony to the faithfulness and the power of Jehovah. It would reassure Elisha's heart of the changeless love of His Lord even as we may reassure ourselves that the Lord, who made a way through Jordan, is none other than Jesus, our Lord, "the same yesterday, today and forever."

Now the day's tour is over, Elijah, the venerable, comes to the end of his journey. He leads his young companion Elisha out a short way into the wilderness that together they might stand and look abroad upon that desert region where God had proved

His faithfulness to His people on so many occasions. Somehow, after visiting these four places of such enshrined memory in the history of God's triumphant dealings with Israel, these two men become themselves memorials of God's faithfulness and their own abiding faith. Then as the evening shadows lengthen across the desert landscape, Elijah steps, like a veteran campaigner who has come to the end of a victorious conquest, into his fiery chariot, and his young companion watches as a mighty whirlwind carries him like an errant star across the darkling blue of the heavens until he is lost to sight. But his career is not over. It is his exile that is at an end for he has returned home. He has been summoned away from amid the ruins and debris of the crumbling national life of his people, and from the smoldering embers of their feeble faith to take his seat of honor in a grander realm and a better world. May the Lord prepare every one of our hearts, as He did that of Elijah, for the day when we shall leave the transient and fleeting things of time and sense in this poor world for that city of gold where glory dwells, where we shall go no more out, where there is fulness of joy and pleasures forevermore.

Chapter XI

ELIJAH — HIS TRANSLATION

"The path of the just is as the shining light that shineth more and more unto the perfect day." The truth of this Scripture was graphically and majestically illustrated to us in the life of Elijah, the Tishbite, whose career we have been following. Although his spiritual fortunes fluctuated in an ever undulating curve of human experience, his entire career was on an ascending plane of colorful glory and ended in a brilliant flash of crowning splendor. We have followed his lonely footsteps all the way from Gilead to Cherith where he camped by the brook, onward to the lonely attic in the widow's home at Zarephath, thence up the sunny slopes of Mt. Carmel, then onward to the hermit cave of Mt. Horeb, pausing with him on the way beneath the shade of the solitary juniper tree. Then we saw him take his successor, Elisha, on an all-day tour of the land, to revisit Gilgal, Bethel, Jericho and Jordan. Thus we have seen that Elijah passes across the scene in a kind of detached manner, more like a brilliant meteor traversing the vault of heaven on a starlit night. We come now to the grand climax of his varied career.

A VETERAN CAMPAIGNER

We have seen the waters of Jordan part to make a way for the two wayfarers, Elijah and Elisha, as they wend their way from Canaan's fair land downwards into the wilderness. When the elder and the younger prophets ascend at the farther bank of Jordan's stream, its murky waters roll on behind them and somehow the two figures are somewhat tragic as they trudge their weary way out across the barren desert. For Elijah, the elder man, earth's links are broken. For him there is no bitter rending of ties that bind him to the earth beneath. To him it is a scene of idolatrous failure, broken covenants, ruined altars and slain prophets. He marches on without a backward look for he has no regrets. He is uniquely the heavenly man and he is going home. His attitude is reminiscent of those matchless words ascribed to all men of faith in the 11th of Hebrews: "And truly, if they had been mindful of that country from whence they came out, they might have had opportunity to have returned, but now they desire a better country, that is, an heavenly; wherefore God is not ashamed to be called their God, for He hath prepared for them a city."

A RAW RECRUIT

The attitude of the younger prophet is very different. He still has work to do here in this world for God. Whereas Elijah, the elder, is like a soldier who has come to the end of a successful campaign, returning home to receive the plaudits of those who love him, Elisha is a raw recruit whose heart beats high in expectation of conquests yet unfought, and he is bent upon catching the secret of the power of the veteran Elijah ere he leaves him. Thus, as we watch these two lone wayfarers journey out beyond Jordan across the trackless waste, they are in earnest conversation together, the younger man expostulating with the elder, evidently seeking to extract some kind of promise in the few remaining moments before the grand translation. The younger soldier has been awed before the brilliant courage, the patient endurance, the uncompromising devotion of the elder. The spirit of Elijah has captivated the young man's heart, and his only concern now is: oh, that he might be endowed with something like that! Suddenly Elijah turns to him and says—*"Ask what I shall do for thee before I be taken away from thee."* And the young man answered *"I pray thee, let a double portion of thy spirit be upon me."* Elijah said—*"Thou hast asked a hard thing. Nevertheless, if thou see me when I am taken from thee it shall be so unto thee; but if not, it shall not be so."*

IN THE WILDERNESS

Onward across the wilderness they went—two lone travellers—across a country so full of remembrance of Jehovah's goodness to His people. It was upon this desert wasteland that the manna had fallen, to be gathered up like coriander seed by the hands of the host of Israel. It was upon this stretch of desert that thousands of wandering feet had left their impress as they had traveled with well-shod feet, and staff in hand under Jehovah's care. Here the water had flowed from the flinty rock to satisfy their thirst. The cloud by day and the pillar of fire by night had been their constant guide and protection. We can well imagine the two prophets standing in the hush of the eventide, and hear again the faint echo of the words of the Lord to Moses — "Thou shalt remember all the way the Lord, thy God, led thee."

THE MIRACLE TAKES PLACE

And, as they stand upon the desert sand, in the deepening shadows of night, the miracle takes place. The silence of the desert evening is suddenly shattered, as though by thunder clash. A mighty chariot of flaming fire drawn by charging horses of brilliant light, emerges from the deepening shadows. It strikes dismay to the heart of the younger man, but it almost seems as if Elijah had been expecting this brilliant intervention. With that quiet dignity and unflinching purpose that had characterized his every movement, he steps with agile willingness into the fiery equipage. The leathern girdle about his loins snaps, and his mantle rolls from off his shoulders at the feet of the younger prophet. In a moment, in the twinkling of an eye, the flaming triumphal car shoots like a meteor across the darkened heavens, while the young man watches in glowing wonder. Elijah is gone! Beyond the gloom and sorrow and disappointments of the earth beneath, with none of the misgivings or fears or anxieties that attach to the article of death, he has been enraptured. No doubt his body was changed in the twinkling of an eye for "flesh and blood cannot inherit the Kingdom of God, neither doth corruption inherit incorruption," but no sense of death's power had gripped his soul as he was translated. Elisha, with that sense of vacancy in his spirit at being parted from his most honored friend, stoops down, picks up the discarded mantle, and stars back on the long trek to bear brilliant testimony to the faith of His Master.

OUR ASCENDED LORD

In this wonderful incident of beauty and power which is so graphically recorded for us in 2nd Kings, chapter 2, we have a wonderful display in type of our blessed Lord Himself. He was in very fact the Heavenly Man. He came from out those ivory palaces of eternal joy and beauty, veiled His glory in spotless incarnation, for He became a Man. "He, being in the form of God, . . . made Himself of no reputation and became in the likeness of men." (Phil. 2:6-7.) For three years of public witness, He passed across this world's dark horizon, with meteoric swiftness and starlight lustre, much like Elijah. The rays of His brilliant light were shed abroad upon the ungrateful heads of all mankind, for His was a light that lighted every man that came into the world. (John 1:9.)

Like Elijah, our Lord knew what it was to be driven forth from the city unwanted. The dried-up brook and the widow's destitution were well-known to Him. He, like Elijah, knew the sunny heights of Carmel's mountain for upon His head the heavens were opened and the Father's voice said: "This is my beloved Son in whom I have found my delight." (Matt. 17:5.) He, too, knew something of the frailty of His spotless humanity and sat betimes under the juniper tree of discouragement, to be strengthened by the kindly hand of Jehovah, His Shepherd. To men His career was a shining light that was ever on the decline, moving onward and downward to reach the depths of darkness and defeat on Calvary's rugged hill, but to the eye of faith He was a conquering Hero. The men who hated Him saw the last of Him on Golgotha's hill, but those who loved Him saw Him risen from the dead in magnificent power.

They journeyed with the Lord one day out yonder as far as Bethany, leaving the proud towers of the doomed city of Jerusalem in the distant haze behind them. His kindly voice of matchless grace re-echoed for the very last time across earth's landscape: "Behold I send the promise of the Father upon you, but tarry ye in the city of Jerusalem until ye be endued with power from high." And, as He stood there, His hands raised in blessing upon their heads, "He was parted from them and carried up into heaven, and they worshipped Him." (Luke 24:51.) That is the brilliant story of the antitype of Elijah, our adorable Saviour.

THE SECRET OF POWER

Just as a double portion of Elijah's spirit fell upon the younger prophet out yonder on the desert beyond Jordan, so the promise of the Spirit came to earth when Jesus was glorified. The Spirit of God on earth is the blessed answer to Christ glorified in heaven. Elijah had said to the young man: "If thou see me when I am taken from thee, but, if not, it shall not be." So it is with the Christian. It is as our eye is fixed upon Christ in glory that the Spirit's power becomes the dynamic of our lives. To see Christ by faith on the cross is the secret of my salvation, but to see Him by faith in the glory is the secret of my power.

Like Elijah, our Lord was cast out, abandoned by this poor world, but He arose from the grave and ascended up in the mighty chariot of the glory of His own finished work, there to sit on the right hand of the majesty on high. As this old world staggers under the weight of many woes, how good to know that Jesus, our Lord, is on the throne. No president has a name so great, no potentate a position so high, no dictator a power so impelling, no king a crown so rich in jewelled splendor, as has the Man of Calvary who is now the Man in the glory. "For we see not yet all things put under Him, but we see Jesus, who was made a little lower than the angels for the suffering of death, crowned with glory and honor." (Heb. 2:8, 9.) The contemplation of this entrances our ravished hearts and we would blend our loud hosannahs to His adorable Name, and crown Him Lord of all. But the crowning day is not yet.

WEARING ELIJAH'S MANTLE

It befits us in the meantime to stoop down low enough, as did Elisha, the younger prophet, out yonder on the barren wilderness, and pick up the mantle of our Master and seek to wear it with some measure of grace and honor in this night of His absence. Elisha's right to wear his master's mantle was his because *He saw him go up.* "If you see me when I am parted from thee." Has our eye of faith yet seen the King in His beauty? First we must see Him by faith at the cross as our sin bearer. But we do not stop there. Let us lift up our eyes and see Him risen and glorified in the heavens. Then in some feeble measure we may wear His mantle. And it is a mantle of grace and power.

When Elisha returned to Canaan by way of Jordan, it was His master's mantle that opened the way once more across Jordan's murky stream. However unworthy you and I may be to wear the mantle of Christ, yet it is only in the power of his risen and endless life that we may journey along a victorious Christian pathway, and enter at long last into those courts of endless glory where Elijah went and where our Saviour sits enthroned.

May the Lord ever give us higher and nobler thoughts of the Christ who died for us, yea rather, that is risen again, who also is at the right hand of God, and whose face we soon shall see!

mountain's position, so high, so distant [illegible] so rich in [illegible] the Man in the [illegible] all [illegible] under Him, but we see Jesus, [illegible] lower than the angels for the suffering of death, [illegible] glory and honor." (Heb. 2:9) [illegible] with our hands and [illegible] His [illegible] Name, and crown Him Lord of all. [illegible] that is not [illegible]

WEARING [illegible]

[illegible]

[illegible]

May the Lord [illegible] Christ [illegible] at the right hand of God [illegible]

ELISHA

Man of Grace

FOREWORD

ELISHA'S name means "God his salvation." It is evident that his ministry of grace brought salvation to countless men and women.

It is interesting to notice the first Biblical reference to this great and kindly prophet. In I Kings 19:16 the Scripture introduces him as "the son of Shaphat of Abelmeholah." Old Testament names always have keen significance. Elisha's father's name, Shaphat, means "judge" and his home locality, Abelmeholah, means "meadow of the dance."

It is not simply incidental that Elisha portrays a character which combines the rectitude and gravity of "the judge" with the blithe spirit of the verdant freshness of "the meadow" and the pastoral symphonic music of "the dance."

There is something joyous about his entire career and, whether he is gazing heavenward as his master, Elijah, is translated, or calling for a minstrel in the dark day of battle and impending defeat, somehow he is ever endearing.

The one reference to Elisha in the New Testament is a peremptory challenge to all: "Many lepers were in Israel in the time of Elisha the prophet; and none of them was cleansed, saving Naaman the Syrian." (Luke 4:27.)

Chapter I

FROM PLOWMAN TO PROPHET

Elisha was one of God's prophets of Old Testament days whose life and actions gave a warm glow of radiant grace to a period of cheerless apathy among God's ancient people. He was the immediate successor to Elijah, a prophet who shone more spectacularly, but not more kindly than the younger man, Elisha.

Both Elijah, the elder prophet, and Elisha, the younger, came upon the world scene at a time of real crisis. The brilliant light of the testimony of God's ancient people Israel had lost its pristine luster, and the gloom of declension and idolatry had overspread the land. Elijah entered the stage of those dramatic days with strident voice and majestic step. Like John the Baptist, who came in the same spirit in the New Testament, Elijah's was a voice crying in the wilderness, calling the people to repentance. The aloofness of the elder prophet challenged the nation to its responsibilities Godward, like a lighthouse on a rocky promontory warning mariners of their peril in the deep, or the brilliant northern star shining serenely above the pounding waves to give the faint-hearted seaman his true course amid the darkness. That was Elijah!

Elisha, his successor, was of different character. If the elder prophet was as the remote lighthouse or the distant guiding star, Elisha was more like the pilot who comes on board during the storm to give help and assurance in kindly grace and guide one safely beyond the danger. Elijah was aloof and distant in his unique ministry; Elisha was close and neighborly.

The two men portray exquisite types of our Lord Himself. Elijah mirrored the beauty of Christ in His place in the heavens, outside the realm of men's scheming; the light of the world calling us to follow Him that we might not walk in darkness but have the light of life. Elisha depicted the Saviour who draws near to our hearts that we might feel the steadying of His hand upon the helm of our lives as we toss and roll in the angry waves of untoward circumstances. The one is characteristically on top of a hill, the other is walking the valley by our side.

Within the pages of the Scriptures as well as in common human experience it is often seen that a man's secular employment before he hears the call of the Lord gives a clue to the character of his service afterward. This is true of Elisha. When first introduced in the Old Testament, Elisha was in the Jordan valley among the undulating hills of that fertile country, and he was a plowman. This gives a key to his spiritual character and his unique ministry. He was a "plowman" to the end, for his patient grace was used of the Lord to send the plowshare of conviction through the rugged heart of his people in those barren days and bring them back to fertility and new life. "He that plougheth should plough in hope" is well borne out in the life of Elisha for his joyous optimism when the going was hard was well demonstrated.

On one occasion, when his enemies were hard upon his heels, and many a man of real faith might have had cause to fear and tremble, Elisha called for a minstrel that his heart, in spite of difficulties, might be attuned to the serenity of heaven. He plowed, and he plowed in hope!

PLOWING IN HOPE

Elisha's career also exemplified our Lord's words in the Gospel of Luke: "No man, having put his hand to the plough, and looking back, is fit for the kingdom of God." There was nothing of the coward about Elisha. He was stalwart and unflinching in his courageous stand for God, yet patient in kindly grace with his brethren. Elisha was always "the plowman."

As a young man, he was in the field following his yoke of oxen, his rough plowshare turning up the brown sod. His was the twelfth yoke of oxen in the field. There were eleven ahead of him, all patiently making their furrows across the good earth. It is not by chance that he was the twelfth in line, for Jehovah has noted the fact on the sacred page for our instruction.

Twelve is ever God's number of full administration of divine goodness through human instrumentality. There were twelve tribes in Israel's national life, twelve disciples and twelve apostles in the New Testament, twelve gates in the heavenly city, twelve thousand furlongs its foursquare measure. (Rev. 21.) Twelve baskets full of fragments were gathered up after the five thousand were fed on the barren desert. (Matt. 14.) Twelve is ever the number associated with God's administration of bounteous blessing as administered through His servants.

Elisha, being the twelfth who followed the plow, was the last of a long line of illustrious servants of God who had spoken in joy and tears, in sunshine and shadow, to this wayward people. Spiritually, they were living in the very last days of their national history. Soon they would be scattered, carried captive, and trodden under foot of the Gentiles. God was raising one last voice to them in Elisha. He was the twelfth plowman and, since we are surely living now in the last days of the dispensation of grace, how needful that we should hear again the voice of Elisha, and allow the plowshare of his patient ministry to turn up the hard and barren soil of our cold hearts that the sunshine of God's grace may again quicken our lukewarm lives.

GOD'S CALL

As Elisha, the plowman, plodded toilsomely across the field a strange sight greeted his eyes. Hard by the hedge-row he came across an aged wayfarer, a great cloak cost about his stooping shoulders. The stranger was Elijah, to whom the Lord had just disclosed that he was about to be taken by fiery chariot to the celestial courts of heaven and that this twelfth plowman was to be his successor.

The elder prophet had reached that unfortunate stage in his spiritual service when he imagined he had outlived his usefulness. The apathetic attitude of his brethren had driven him out from among them, and he had been sitting in the shade of a juniper tree, his heart filled with self-pity because he was not appreciated. He wished that the Lord would take him away. Then he had gone to the lone cave on Mount Horeb to become a hermit, for it all seemed so useless. There, in spectacular drama, Jehovah had shown him that He could use whirlwind, earthquake or flashing fire, but that He had chosen to use His servant merely as a still, small voice.

Now Elijah's term of service was over. He was to be promoted to heaven, and another was to be appointed to his arduous task on earth. Elisha, the plowman, was to be that successor. As Elisha came near, Elijah took the cloak from his own shoulders and cast it about the younger man. It was a symbolic gesture. This was God's call to the young man, telling him that Jehovah had other fields for him to plow, even the hearts of his own people Israel. He stopped the plow, unhitched the yoke of oxen and hastened back to the farmhouse on the hill.

FINISHED WITH THE OLD

It must have been a great event in the life of this young man, even as it is a great event in our lives when first we hear God's call echo through the channels of our soul. Elisha's friends and neighbors were assembled; a great feast was spread. With lavish hand he demonstrated to all that he was making a great change. It was both a celebration and a confession. Everyone had to be told that he had been called to a better service and that he had a new master.

Elisha took the oxen with which he had been plowing the field, slew them and served them at the feast of celebration. It was his way of declaring that he was no longer going to have any use for these things which represented the old way of life and all its associations. He was beginning a new career for God and there was going to be no compromise with the past.

What a testimony this should bear to all in this day! When God calls us, He wants us for Himself alone. He will not share the place of ascendency in our hearts with any other. When we confess Jesus as Lord, there must be a clean break with the old life. We must "boil the old oxen" so that there will be no temptation for us to return to that world in which we lived without Christ. We must burn our bridges behind us. We must go three days' journey out of Egypt, separated from its fleshpots and its sin by the rolling waters of the sea of death. That is precisely what Elisha did, and it is what we must do if we are going to enjoy the salvation of the Lord.

Far too many people accept Christ as a kind of addition to their old life; a change of thought and ideas. God wants men to turn from darkness to light and from the power of Satan to God; to turn us "from idols to serve the living and true God and to wait for His Son from heaven." What we need is clean-cut conversion. Then only shall we, like Elisha, go forth in the power of our Master, wearing the blessed mantle of the Saviour in grace and power.

The man who confesses Christ as Lord in uncompromising grace before his fellows and makes a new start, dependent on the Saviour who shed His blood to save him, will not be disappointed.

Chapter II

HIS MASTER'S MANTLE

We observe that episode in the story of Elisha recorded for us in 1 Kings 19, that he was plowing in the field, and he was the *last* plowman in a long line of twelve. Elijah found him there, and cast his mantle upon Elisha's young shoulders, thus initiating him into the ministry in which he was yet to shine so faithfully.

THE LAST PLOWMAN

This is a reminder to us that it is ever the Lord's way to make the last first, to take up the most unlikely of us for His service; "for ye see your calling brethren, how that not many wise men after the flesh, not many mighty, not many noble, are called. But God hath chosen the foolish things of the world to confound the wise; and God hath chosen the weak things of the world to confound the things that are mighty . . . that no flesh should glory in his presence." (1 Cor. 1:27-29.)

Man would have chosen the plowman who led the field with the best yoke of oxen, but God selected Elisha the twelfth and last. Thus God takes up those whom men have discounted "that in the ages to come He might shew the exceeding riches of His grace in His kindness towards us through Christ Jesus." (Eph. 1:7.)

If we are Christians, God did not confer that honor upon us because we exhibited possibilities as men in the flesh. He did not choose us because we had the background that would add color to our present service for Him. He chose us because His great heart of love yearned to bless us, and to fit us by His matchless grace to be in the honored company that will shine in the heavenly kingdom.

THROUGH JORDAN

When Elisha was chosen by the elder prophet, Elijah's mantle was put upon him, and he became a follower of his revered master. Indeed Elijah's mantle played no small part in the initial life of service of the younger prophet. Without it he would have been discarded in the first place, and defeated a little later.

The story is again taken up in 2 Kings 2, where the two men had just finished making an all-day tour of the countryside so sacred in the memory of Israel's history. They had visited the national shrines of Gilgal, Bethel, then out to Jericho, and finally back across the river Jordan. As they came to the muddy stream, it must have seemed like an impassable barrier to the younger prophet as he trudged along side by side with his master. But the elder hesitated at the brink of the murky waters only long enough to slip his cloak from his shoulders. He raised the honored mantle above his head and brought it down with a will upon the stream. It clove the river like a plowshare, opening a furrow that reached miraculously across the depths, leaving a highway across which the two men walked dryshod.

How young Elisha must have looked at that mantle! This was the second time it had played a part in his young life, first calling him from the plow to follow Elijah, and now parting the dark waters of the Jordan at their feet.

THE TRANSLATION

The two men passed over to the wilderness side, leaving behind the fair land of Canaan, where their people dwelt under God's favor, yet in sad dejection and unfaithfulness to their Lord. The cold waters of the Jordan rolled back after they had passed over, and they traveled together across the barren wasteland. No doubt Elisha eyed that mantle many times. Would a day come when he would be worthy to wear that cloak of symbolic beauty and power? He knew well that he could never measure up to the moral graces of his master.

As these thoughts coursed through his heart and mind, suddenly Elijah turned to him. Almost as though he had read Elisha's thoughts, he said: "Ask what I shall do for thee, before I be taken from thee." And the young man said: "I pray thee, let a double portion of thy spirit be upon me." So unworthy did he feel that he knew that only a double portion of the same spirit would suffice for him. Elijah said: "Thou hast asked a hard thing; nevertheless, if thou see me when I am taken from thee, it shall be so unto thee, but if not, it shall not be so."

No sooner were the words spoken than the chariot of fire appeared. Like a bolt from heaven in the gathering shadows of the evening it descended, horses of fire charging through the clouds, living sparks of flame flashing from their heels. The elder prophet was caught up by the accompanying whirlwind and transported heavenward as Elisha stood transfixed in holy wonder at the sight. Like a meteor shot from the bow of the Almighty, the chariot ascended the heavens and was lost in the infinite depths of limitless space.

Elisha watched the grand translation, just as his master had told him it would be. The earth must have seemed very vacant to him then. Perhaps we, too, have known that same feeling of vacancy that seized the young man's heart. We may have known it as we stood on the docks waving goodbye to a loved one outward bound across the ocean. Or we may have felt it as we stood at the bedside of a loved one and watched death's shadows descend in awesome and relentless power. This was the feeling Elisha experienced as his master was parted from him.

"IF THOU SEE ME TAKEN UP"

Elisha must have looked long and lingeringly at the vanishing wake of the fiery chariot. Then, as his eyes and thoughts returned to earth, his bewildered gaze fell upon something that lay at his feet. He stooped down low to pick it up. A leathern girdle and a cloak! Then he remembered. This was Elijah's cloak.

It had fallen from the prophet's shoulders as he was enraptured. But Elisha could never wear *that* mantle! He was unworthy. He had never felt so unworthy as now. He could never put that mantle about himself until he had cultivated the spirit of grace and power in which his master had walked so nobly across the earth.

Then Elijah's words came back to him. *"If thou see me when I am taken from thee."* Elisha had seen him! He had watched with longing eyes and enraptured heart as his master made the grand ascent of the heavens. He had fulfilled the condition. Surely Elijah would keep his word. Elisha believed it, and he swung the mantle with easy grace across his shoulders. He had a right to wear it! Thus arrayed, he started back towards Canaan for he had much work to do; but soon after he was put to the test.

All this had been very spectacular, and it must have been in much bewilderment that Elisha traveled back across the lonely desert, deeply absorbed in what he had just witnessed. Soon he came to the Jordan's impassable barrier. How was he to get across it now? It had been simple before when Elijah had been with him. But now he was alone. Then he recalled how the elder prophet had taken his mantle and had struck the waters with it so that they parted asunder. He did not have Elijah, but he did have the mantle, and off it came from his back. He brought it down upon the forbidding waters. They parted! It worked! As Elisha crossed the stream dryshod, he must have envisioned his master, in exaltation in the heavens, yet with an eye on him there in the valley.

THE BEST ROBE

Thus we see how unique a place this mantle of Elijah had in the early experiences of Elisha. It was that by which he was first called by God into His service, and that in which he walked thereafter in grace and power. How graphically symbolic it is of the dress in which every one of the redeemed is arrayed by God's grace.

This recalls to our hearts the wonderful story of the prodigal returning from the place of distance, of sin and shame in the far country, coming out of the shadows of his rebellion and misery to hear the glad voice of his father: "Bring forth the best robe and put it on him." (Luke 15:22.) It is the righteousness of God in Christ for every sinner. It is our Lord's mantle of acceptability put upon our unworthy shoulders. It is the work of the Cross on our behalf where Jesus the Saviour died, the just for the unjust, to bring us to God. It is the wedding garment of honor to the bridegroom without which we would be cast into outer darkness. That is the first aspect of our Lord's mantle, but there is another also.

"POWER FROM ON HIGH"

Elisha was called, but he needed grace and power to walk for God after his master was enraptured to heaven. For this he got two things: a double portion of his master's spirit, and his master's mantle to adorn his walk. When Jesus the Lord went up on high, His promise was that He would send the Holy Spirit down to indwell His people. "Behold I send the promise of the Father upon you, but tarry ye in Jerusalem until ye be endued with power from on high." (Luke 24:49.)

The Spirit of God, the third Person of the Trinity, came to earth at Pentecost, and He has been here ever since, indwelling the hearts of all believers. He is here as our Comforter to conduct us homeward in the power of brilliant testimony. His power in each one of His people is commensurate with our occupation with Christ on high. "If you see me when I am taken from you" was Elijah's condition to Elisha, and to us it is, "We all, with open face beholding as in a glass the glory of the Lord, are changed into the same image from glory to glory, even as by the Spirit of the Lord."

Chapter III

SALT IN A NEW CRUSE

Pictures and photographs are but an artistic blending of lights and shadows. The beauty of the picture will be appreciated only by those who have eyes to see the harmonious blending of these lights and shadows. The Bible is God's picture book, but none can see the artistry of these divine masterpieces which the Lord has painted upon the homespun canvas of the common-place until their vision has been sharpened to discern both the lights and the shadows. The men of the Old Testament are the shadows, and they will seem but drab and colorless unless we see them blended with the true light of their great Antitype, Jesus our Lord.

If we want to know the Old Testament as a book of fascinating pictures, we must let the light of Christ illumine its shadowy figures. Men like Elisha, when their Antitype is known, will spring to life with colorful beauty, and their careers will become dramatic, real and shining with moral grandeur.

JERICHO

After bidding farewell to Elijah at his spectacular translation, Elisha had come back across the Jordan. He had smitten the river Jordan with his master's mantle, and it had walled its waters to make a dry highway for the returning pilgrim. Having crossed the stream, he made directly for one of the nearest towns—Jericho.

Jericho! What visions that name arouses in one's mind. To one who knows its place in the pageant of Bible history, the name brings vivid recollections. In the New Testament, blind Bartimeus sat begging outside its gates as Jesus passed that way. It was on the highway from Jerusalem to Jericho that the good Samaritan found the man who had fallen among thieves, bound up his wounds and carried him to the city inn to be tended. In the Old Testament, the story of Jericho is just as dramatic. Its name meant "fragrance," but when Elisha came to tarry there Jericho's appearance belied its name. It was then a barren wasteland.

Jericho, however, had not always been a desolate land. There was the time when Moses had quietly made the ascent of Mount Pisgah that he might look across the Jordan to the promised land of Canaan on which Jehovah had told him he would never set foot. He was about to lie down and die, for his career was over, but, as he stood on the mountain, how longingly he gazed across the river. Moses saw the murky Jordan and just beyond lay Jericho, surrounded by fair and fertile valleys exuberant with luscious verdure; its streets lined with palms. Jericho's name meant "fragrance" then, and it was called "the city of palm trees."

But things had changed since Moses' time. Jericho had become a fastness of defense against God's people and a stronghold of their enemies. Then Joshua and his host, by miraculous power, had besieged it with trumpet blast and laid it waste. Since then, Jericho had been rebuilt but its grandeur was gone, and Elisha found it a sorry prospect. When he arrived at Jericho, the man of God found it characterized by four very unfavorable elements. As stated in 2 Kings 2, he found *unbelief, bitterness, barrenness* and *mockery;* but Elisha had a remedy for each of them.

UNBELIEF

We must remember that Elisha typifies the Christian in his life of testimony to his ascended Lord. The first people Elisha met in Jericho were what might be called religious unbelievers, and this type are legion even today. Fifty of the sons of the prophets met him, but they would not believe that his master, Elijah, was alive and gone to heaven. They insisted on making a three-day search for him among the hills and valleys where they believed he must lie dead. Their search, of course, was useless. Yet, in spite of their unbelief, they were so impressed by the testimony of Elisha that they bowed to the ground before the young prophet.

There are many like these unbelievers today; men who have religion in their lives but who do not believe in a living and glorified Saviour. They admit that Jesus our Lord was a wonderful Man, but they speak of Him in the past tense.

OUR RISEN LORD

Do we believe that Jesus is alive? Our eternal salvation depends on it. "If thou shalt confess with thy mouth Jesus as Lord, and believe in thine heart that God hath raised Him from the dead, thou shalt be saved." May we who are Christians be more like Elisha and live in the light of our ascended Lord, a living, glorified Man in the presence of God now! That was Elisha's cure for the first ill, *unbelief,* and it is our cure also, for the gospel is the power of God unto salvation still.

BITTERNESS AND BARRENNESS

We should take special notice of Elisha's cure for the next two elements. In Jericho, he found not only unbelief, but *bitterness* and *barrenness* as well. The streams were foul and bitter. The land, where palm trees once waved in splendor, where flowers had bloomed in abundance and grass had grown in luxuriant beauty, was all barren now. Desolation lay across the once fertile valleys like a blighting plague, and the streams were polluted with grievous bitterness.

The description might also depict our world of today. This present creation, which was once so fair and full of fragrant beauty, has become despoiled by sin. The whole creation groans and travails, and the blackest stain is the darkness of the human heart blighted by sin. "By one man sin entered into the world and death by sin."

As we look across the world today, what a spectacle of barrenness it presents! The once rippling streams of sparkling refreshment have become bitter with disappointment, heartache, sorrow, bereavement, and by the blight of death itself. Man's life, instead of being devoted to helpfulness, love, the pursuit of happiness for himself and others, has become barren and unfruitful. Instead of growing things, he is destroying them. Instead of spreading life and healing, he is destroying.

THE NEW CRUSE

Such is the picture of the Jericho of the present century, and it may profit us to inquire diligently as to what Elisha did about it in his day. Therein we may find the remedy for our present tragic state.

Elisha got a new cruse and put salt in it, and carried it up into the hills until he found the source of the streams. There he poured in the salt, and the waters became sweet. The land, fed by their limpid freshness, became fruitful and abundant again. It was a strange remedy! The salt counteracted the poison in the polluted streams, and they became living and life-giving; the barrenness turned to abundance.

How wonderful is the Antitype! A new cruse with salt in it. Surely this points directly to the Son of God Himself as John the Apostle described Him. There we see a vessel, a new cruse. Earth had never seen its like. It came down from heaven. "The Lord became flesh and dwelt among us." He was a vessel of a new order. He was Immanuel, "God with us."

"And we beheld His glory, the glory as of an only begotten with a father, full of grace and truth." Notice that — "full of grace and truth." The vessel had *salt* in it! Those two elements which alone could counteract the bitterness of earth's polluted streams, *grace* and *truth.*

The incarnate Son of God came to earth, right to the source of all men's trouble. He took up the question of sin at its source and settled it forever. This was the remedy Elisha carried in his day, and it made the bitter sweet; the barren fruitful. It is the same new cruse filled with salt, the testimony of Jesus the Son of God, that comes to us in the gospel. If we take Him into our lives, allow His grace and truth to touch us in the moral springs of our being, He will make us whole. He said: "I am come that ye might have life, and that ye might have it abundantly." And, "He that believeth on me, out of his belly shall flow rivers of living water."

Our life loses its bitterness and its sin in the same measure in which we allow the Lord to control us. In this way many people have exchanged a life of shame, disappointment, unworthiness and hard unbelief for a life of peace and fruitfulness for themselves and others also.

MOCKERY

Then there was the last unfavorable element which Elisha found in the city of Jericho. These were the mockers, and Elisha had a remedy for them also. They crowded him on the street, laughed him to scorn, called him a "bald head," and indicated that the sooner he followed his master up to heaven the better they would be suited.

There are many such in the world today. They mock at our Saviour, our ascended Lord, and indicate in no uncertain terms that the sooner we get out the better. Of course not all unbelievers are mockers, but there are many of them even as the Apostle Jude said there would be in the last times.

SWIFT JUDGMENT

Elisha's treatment of the mockers was swift and sure. No kindly grace for them! He cursed them in the Name of the Lord, and she-bears came out of the wood and destroyed them.

Swift judgment is God's answer to man's mockery. We must not trifle with the living God Who has said: "Because I have called and ye refused; I have stretched out my hand and no man regarded. Ye have set at naught all my counsel, and would none of my reproof; I also will laugh at your calamity. I will mock when your fear cometh. Then shall they call upon me, but I will not answer; they shall seek me early, but shall not find me." But He says in the same first chapter of Proverbs: "Whoso hearkeneth unto me shall dwell safely."

GOD'S REMEDY

Through this wonderful story of Elisha the prophet in Jericho, we see God's present remedy for all our ills. His gospel presents salvation as the cure for our unbelief. The new cruse filled with salt, Jesus the new vessel come down from heaven to bring the sweetness of grace and truth to us, is God's remedy for the bitterness and barrenness in our lives. If we mock at His offer of mercy, there remains only judgment swift and sure.

"He that believeth on the Son hath everlasting life; and he that believeth not the Son shall not see life, but the wrath of God abideth on Him."

Chapter IV

BRING ME A MINSTREL

The story of Elisha the prophet and the people among whom he lived, as related in 2 Kings 3, might be a page from the book of our own modern life. It presents to us with graphic, picturesque color the remarkable history of God's ancient people, weakened by disunity and compromise with evil, and their restoration to a life of harmony and nearness to Jehovah.

The people of God were divided then, even as they are in our day. Judah and Israel stood in juxtaposition to each other, with a wicked king ruling over Israel and a cowardly, although pious, monarch on the throne of Judah. In order to strengthen their complex position, they jointly made an unholy alliance with a heathen potentate and their three armies marched together against the Moabites, their common enemy.

For the first time in his ungodly life, Israel's wicked king trembled in his shoes and wondered if Jehovah might have caught up with him at long last and determined upon his destruction. It was then that Elisha the prophet was called in, and he stepped upon the scene in the majesty of his holy calling.

A FALSE UNITY

How closely akin is all of this to life in our modern world! The people of God, like a house divided against itself, are made conscious today of their own spiritual weakness. Their misguided leaders have often sought to gather strength by unholy alliances with unbelievers around them. Like Jehoshaphat, Judah's king, who was pious at heart, they have compromised by joining hands with those who profess godliness, but deny its power, and they have reached out even further to add to their ranks those who are openly hostile to the truth of God. Thus we have three armies marching shoulder to shoulder in a false unity; the church, the world and the devil, and the true man of God must stand apart from it all as did Elisha. And one may be sure that, when the well-laid plans of men go awry, they will look over their shoulders as they did in Elisha's day, to see if they can find a true man of God who will come forward with a solution to their perilous difficulties.

Chracteristically, the three kings had left Elisha out of their proud scheming, but he drew graciously near when they needed him. Their three armies were assembled in the valley, and yonder was the mighty, unified army of their enemies, the Moabites, ready to swoop down in unrelenting power to destroy them.

A DEFEATED ARMY

It was a critical moment in which the three kings—the ungodly ruler of Israel, the heathen king of Edom, and the pious monarch of Judah—drew near to Elisha. It was a time for swift action and no one knew it better than did God's prophet. The tide of circumstance was against them. The three armies had been assembled in that valley for some time, and they were without water. There was no reservoir from which they could draw new supplies. It was but a matter of time until the armies would succumb to agonizing thirst, and it would be child's play for the Moabites to descend and destroy them to the last man. The valley below was a barren, arid desert. There was not a sign of a cloud in the sky. Not a bush stirred in the wind. The overhanging silence and stillness had the portent of unrelenting drought. The three kings observed all this and, in the last extremity of their need, appealed urgently to Elisha for his advice.

Elisha told the ungodly Israelite that he would not even deign to look upon him were it not for the presence of the pious Jehosphat, King of Judah. Elisha was no smooth talker. He had no wish to gloss over the truth. He knew the Israelite king had been wicked and arrogant, and that he should have been destroyed were it not for the mercy of God. The only fact that might excuse the ungodly king was that his father, Ahab, and his mother, Jezebel, had been even more infamous than he was.

ELISHA'S ADVICE

Elisha stood there as a kind of super-strategist, scanning the battlefield. Had he not been a true man of God, he might have laid out a specific plan of attack, ranging the already depleted armies upon strategic sides of the great valley so that they could make flanking attacks upon their enemy. Elisha did not do that. His move was of a most surprising character and quite unsoldier-like. The three kings must have been startled indeed when he said, *"Bring me a minstrel!"*

What a strange command at a time of crisis when the armies

of his people stood on the brink of destruction! "Bring me a minstrel!" Of all the unmitigated folly on the day of battle, surely this was the climax! Was he a doted old man who had become childish in his feeble years? No, Elisha was a young man; bright, alert, with a full appreciation of all the critical elements that weighed in the balance of this perilous hour. "Bring me a minstrel," he said. The minstrel came, and the sound of the harp and the long-forgotten songs of Zion carried across the stillness of the valley.

THE JOY OF THE LORD

One can imagine the tired, weary and thirsty warriors, leaning dejectedly upon their swords, and visualize them pricking their ears suddenly like watch dogs to catch the harmonious strain of the minstrel's song as its enchanting melody wafted across the barren waste. One might think of Elisha as a kind of Nero fiddling while Rome burned, but it was not so. The man of God knew that the people whom he loved so much were out of harmony with the Lord, and that only the reverberation of the songs of Zion would bring their hearts back in tune with their God and strengthen their courage. It was Elisha's way of telling them that the joy of the Lord was their strength. They had lost their joy, and with it had gone their fighting qualities.

Surely the truth of this comes home to us. Many of God's people have lingering memories that carry them back to sweeter days when they sang the songs of the redeemed. They remember when they sang such heavenly melodies as the song called "Jewels," a line of which says, "like the stars of the morning, His bright crown adorning, they shall shine in their beauty, bright gems for His crown." They remember when their voices woke the echoes of the morning, singing praise to the Lord with whom they walked so closely. But dark days came, and they hung their harps on the willows and settled down in a valley of impotence and unhappy forgetfulness of their Redeemer. The sun sank low over yonder hill, and they sat in the shadows, the sense of nearness to their Lord went out of their hearts and their song was no longer heard. Little wonder they ceased to be soldiers for Christ and leaned in impotence upon their swords. "Bring me a minstrel!"

Let us remember that God Himself has sent a heavenly minstrel into this world in the person of the Holy Spirit that we might have "joy in the Holy Ghost." Joy is one of the fruits of the Spirit, and it is only as His divine fingers touch the trembling chords of our hearts that they shall well forth with the songs of Zion. Let us take down our harps and finger them with the kindly grace once so dear to us. We may think the days are too dark for that. Remember Elisha, who stood face to face with three compromising kings in a scene of desolation, weakness and spiritual poverty. Everything was against them. Not a ray of hope was visible to the eye. "Bring me a minstrel," said Elisha. The Minstrel is here and waiting upon us in our day. He longs to carry us to the courts of glory on the wings of His melody in order that our hearts might rejoice, and that our lives, so out of tune, might be brought back into harmony with the Lord. If we have wandered away, let us turn back.

LET EVERY MAN DIG

But the Lord would remind us, even as Elisha reminded the kings, that the path of faith is not always a joyous experience, set to music. A song alone did not remove the difficulties of these three armies as they sat there on the barren desert wondering how soon the Moabites would fall upon them to their destruction. They were not only unhappy, but they were also thirsty, and there was no water in the valley. We may be sure that, when our lives get out of harmony with the Lord, when our song is stilled and our harps are laid aside, the refreshing streams which once flowed in such limpid grace through the channels of our souls will be dried up and our hearts will be barren and thirsty. The armies of the three kings needed melody in their spirits, but they needed water to quench their thirst.

Then Elisha said, "Make the valley full of ditches, let every man dig." Was this another foolhardy notion, spun from the doted mind of a religious dreamer? Neither wind nor cloud were in evidence; there was no sign of rain anywhere. There were no evidences of springs in that valley, for it was a wilderness. What was the use, then, of digging ditches? But the man of God knew his business well. He had brought melody back into the soldiers' hearts and their spirits were lifted. "Now," he said, "dig!"

DRY DITCHES

The vast army of men got to their feet. Their swords became spades, and each man, precisely where he was, began to dig. They continued through the day, and probably through the night. It must have seemed a fruitless task. The hours rolled by with no sign of water. The whole valley became filled with dry ditches. Was this some scheme of mockery which Elisha was trying to foist upon the kings because of their ungodliness?

Morning came. The sun's golden disk crept above the horizon, flooding the valley with its kindly light. Then, true to the tradition of their faith in God, the people were assembled for morning worship. The sacrifice of meal was brought and offered to Jehovah at the hour of sunrise. It must have seemed a feeble gesture on the part of an army that had abandoned its warlike character to become a host of ditch diggers. Why take time out for the offering of meal on the day when, in all probability, they should be slain? What a waste of time! But this was Elisha's way of reminding them that they were still under the watchful eye of Jehovah.

LIVING WATER

The sacrifice of meal was offered up; and then it came! Up yonder at the top of the valley, where the sheltering hills on either side came closest together, they saw it come! Whence it came they could not tell, but it was real water; flowing, cascading, tumbling in full abundance, down through the valley, filling all the ditches in its course. It seemed as though a mighty dam had broken loose, flooding the valley with living streams. They could hardly believe their eyes as it tore down across the valley in torrents. And a host of warriors, upon their knees, drank from the living streams and slaked their parched throats to satisfaction.

This was what Elisha had foreseen when he commanded them to dig. If our lives are out of harmony with the Lord, we need to do two things. We need to summon the Minstrel, who is the Holy Spirit, to revivify our drooping spirits and fill our hearts again with the joy of heaven so that we break forth in songs of gladness. Let us get out the hymn book and sing the songs of the redeemed.

LET US REJOICE

Then let us take that sword, long idle, and start to dig. Beginning right at our own feet, let us clear away the dust and rubbish that has accumulated through the years; all the speculative debris of our own unbelief. Let us not take time to look around at the deficiencies of others. Never mind the unholy alliance—the union of the church and the world. Let us clear the channels of mind and heart for the inflow of God's goodness.

As the night rolls on and the light of morning begins to dawn in our souls, let us remember the offering. The meal offering used by Elisha symbolically setting forth the excellencies of Christ, our Saviour. It was the sacrifice of His own perfect manhood, offered up as a morning oblation to Jehovah. Let the glories of His Person, the majesty of His beauty, the excellencies of His Name go up from our thankful hearts to Jehovah. The water will come cascading down the slopes of heaven's hills, right into the ditches at our very feet, so that we can stoop down and drink. Then shall we sing again, "I came to Jesus and I drank of that life-giving stream. My thirst was quenched, my soul revived, and now I live in Him."

Such was the road to victory in Elisha's day and it will lead us to triumph also. The water that quenched the thirst of Israel's rejoicing armies glistened so brightly in the sun that their enemies thought it was blood covering the landscape. They came over, prepared to finish off the remnant of their broken foe, but found instead an army of stout, happy warriors who met them in victorious combat.

Chapter V

THE WIDOW'S CRUSE OF OIL

In the opening of the fourth chapter of the Second Book of Kings there is a domestic scene which presents to us in impelling drama one of the most graphic illustrations of the gospel of God's grace to be found in all the Bible.

The story introduces us to a scene of poverty in the home of a destitute widow. She had been the wife of the son of one of the prophets, but he was dead and with him had gone her wealth. She had evidently sold her belongings, but the proceeds from them had been insufficient to pay her debts. Now the creditor was knocking urgently upon the door of her humble dwelling, demanding a reckoning of their account, and threatening to take her two sons into slavery to pay their charges.

THE CREDITOR'S KNOCK

But as the resounding knock of the creditor is heard upon the door of this woman's humble domicile, the voice of another breaks in upon the tragic drama. It is the voice of Elisha, whose name means *"God is salvation."* Elisha is the man of grace; he hears the appeal of the destitute woman, and he asks her a strange question. He says, "What hast thou in the house?"

She answers, "Thine handmaid hath not anything in the house save a pot of oil." From attic to cellar the house had been bereft of its furnishings. Since that fateful day when death struck, evidently everything had been sold in an effort to meet the increasing demands of the creditors. Yet there stood within the home a worthless vessel, besmirched and neglected, of no evident value to anyone. In it there was some olive oil which was so plentiful in that land of green olive trees that no one thought it worth while to take it. Only an Elisha knew its value! He knew how far a little olive oil would go under the almighty hand of the Lord, and that the unworthy earthen vessel which stood neglected in the corner of the empty house held within its compass the solution of all this woman's difficulties.

We might ask ourselves the question which was propounded by Elisha to this destitute woman. "What have you in the house?" We know that there lies close to our hand within the empty chamber of our own spiritual poverty an "earthen vessel" long neglected, probably unnoticed for years, yet it is an "earthen vessel" filled with divine grace that is sufficient to meet our deepest needs. That "earthen vessel" is Jesus Christ, our Lord. His Name, so precious in the heavens, is besmirched and begrimed by man's disdain. "He is despised and rejected of men; a man of sorrows and acquainted with grief." As an "earthen vessel" He was so ordinary in appearance that men said: "There is no beauty in Him that we should desire Him." He had no negotiable value, as it were, in their estimation. When the proud Pharisees came upon Him, they curled the lip in disdain. Yet in that blessed "earthen vessel" is the oil of divine grace. Have we relegated Him to some neglected corner of our dwelling, forgotten and counted worthless in our life's reckoning?

THE PRECIOUS OIL

How emblematic is this "olive oil in the earthen vessel" of the Son of God become flesh, bringing the wealth of heaven's healing balm into a sin-sick world! He it was who could say: "I am like a green olive tree in the house of my God." Olive oil may seem a very ordinary commodity in a land where it is plentiful, and the grace of God may seem very ordinary to us because we live in a land where the Gospel of grace is declared on every hand. But let us remember that the fruit of that green olive tree had to be plucked; it had to be put into a press and crushed in order that the oil might flow forth in abundance.

The Lord of Glory had to come down here into this world, and go all the way to Calvary. There He was crushed under the upper and the nether millstones of the judgment of a Holy God, and the hatred of His creature man, in order that divine grace in efficacious power might flow out to all mankind.

Because Elisha knew the value of that vessel of oil in the bankrupt home, it became the most precious treasure in the widow's life. "Unto us who believe He is precious!"

Elisha told the widow: "Go borrow thee vessels abroad of all thy neighbors, empty vessels, borrow not a few. And when thou art come in, thou shalt shut the door upon thee and upon thy sons, and shall pour into all those vessels and thou shall set aside that which is full." And so she poured. When all the vessels were full, she said to her son, "Bring me yet a vessel." And he said, "There is not a vessel more." Then the oil stayed.

We can well imagine this woman sending her two sons out through the neighborhood that day, to call at all the houses and ask for empty vessels. It mattered not what kind of vessel it might be; so long as it was empty it was a proper receptacle for the oil. Through the streets and lanes of the city, out into the highways and the hedges the two sons went to gather empty vessels. Big ones, little ones, golden vessels as well as stone jars; beautifully decorated vessels as well as the plain, ordinary ones. They were all gathered together, from the mansions on the hillside and from the dunghill outside the gate. Then she began to pour. One after another the empty vessels were filled. Notice that the man of God had specified that they must be *empty* vessels. Any vessel which had anything in it would have to be rejected; but every empty vessel was filled.

GRACE SUPER-ABOUNDS

How wonderfully emblematic of the gospel of grace in our day. If we will empty ourselves of our own self-righteousness, if we will lay aside our own efforts toward salvation, ceasing to bring our own merits, and just come as empty vessels, then the oil will be poured in. If we come to Christ without reservation, He will save us, for He is "the same Lord over all, rich unto all that call upon Him, and whosoever shall call upon the Name of the Lord shall be saved."

Thus the widow kept filling, and the young men kept bringing empty vessels. There was no let-up of the oil. A superabundance was poured forth from that earthen vessel. There is a superabundance of grace in Christ. No matter how black our sin, however disgraceful our past life, however proud and arrogant we may have been, however we have boasted in our own self-righteousness and despised and rejected Jesus, the Son of God, "where sin abounds, grace doth much more abound."

As the widow poured, the vessels were filled, until she came to the last one and then she called out to her son," Bring another vessel." The lad told her there were no more empty ones, and then the oil stopped. God has warned us not to neglect so great salvation. He has told us that "now is the accepted time." Someone will be the last to accept the opportunity to be filled with God's grace.

LIVE ON THE SURPLUS

There is an interesting touch in the close of this story. The destitute widow found that the oil, which had come to her through the man of God, was sufficient to pay all her debts, and she was able to live on the surplus. God's grace not only can, but it has, paid all our debts. When Christ took our place on Calvary's Cross, He bore our sins in His own body on the Tree, and through His Name we are now justified from all things. "Jesus paid it all, all to Him I owe, sin had left a crimson stain, He washed it white as snow." And the same grace that saved us, is able to keep us. Like the woman, we can live on the surplus, on the lavish abundance of the wealth of God's providing.

How wonderful is the grace of God that meets all our needs, brings us into eternal relationship with God, our Father, in and through our Lord Jesus Christ, and gives us the joy of the Holy Spirit to gladden our hearts eternally. "For ye know the grace of our Lord Jesus Christ, that, tho' He was rich, yet for your sakes He became poor, that ye through His poverty might be rich." (2 Cor. 8:9.)

Chapter VI

THE SHUNAMMITE FROM PATRONAGE TO WORSHIP

The Bible is a book of striking contrasts. This is graphically illustrated in the life of Elisha, the prophet. In 2 Kings 4, we have the story of the enrichment of the destitute widow whose accumulated debts threatened the enslavement of her two sons by an unrelenting creditor. The widow's plight was great indeed, but the man of God found a solution to all her problems in the pot of oil that stood neglected in her impoverished dwelling. Thus Elisha turned abject poverty into abundant wealth and joy, even as Christ our Redeemer has made those who trust in Him rich with eternal riches.

"A GREAT WOMAN"

It may seem rather strange that, right in the same chapter, the very next person brought before us is, in striking contrast, a wealthy lady of prominence, of dignity and social distinction. But she had a problem just as real as that of the destitute widow, and Elisha had the key to its solution as well. From the story, one would judge the lady lived in a grand villa that stood in imposing grace near the highway that led from the great city down to the smaller town of Shunem. Elisha often passed that way, and the lady had seen the unpretentious wayfarer as he took his weary journey along the dusty highway past her window. Soon the lady of high distinction deigned to notice the stranger more carefully. Her scant acquaintance impressed her greatly, and she mentioned him to her husband as "a holy man of God."

There seemed to be no particular disdain in the title, neither was there much admiration, for she was a great lady and Elisha was only a prophet in days when godliness was in the discard. But the "great woman" took kindly to Elisha and she decided to patronize him and show him generosity. It would hardly do to invite him into her proud mansion, for so humble a man would not grace her living room. There was "a little chamber," however, by the wall of her house. She bade him step in there and rest before going on his way on his frequent journeys to and from Shunem. Her benevolence did not accord the stranger the run of her home, but in the chamber by the wall she provided a few necessities for his accommodation, *a bed, a table, a stool, and a candlestick.* They were not much, but he was an unpretentious person, and no doubt glad of such simple hospitality. Thus the "man of God" was patronized by the proud and wealthy lady whose heart had been just a little touched by Elisha's grace and dignified holiness.

There had been no such restraint in the welcome given Elisha by the former widow in the same chapter, but she needed him much, and this woman was "a great woman." However, the man of God appreciated her kindness and took the guest chamber assigned to him. What else could he do? He was not popular except among those who really loved his Lord, but they were few and far between. After all, it was all he needed.

"A ROOM FURNISHED"

We cannot pass by the mention of the furnishings provided in this spare room without seeing how graphically they tell of the provision which our Lord has made for each of His children as they journey along the dusty roads of time's desert landscape. A *walled chamber* reminds us all of the dwelling so secure into which God has brought His people, sheltered by the sure protection of His almighty power. "He that dwelleth in the secret place of the most High shall abide under the shadow of the Almighty." In that sure dwelling, He has provided for us *a bed,* where we may rest from anxiety and fear; *a table,* where we may sit with Him and enjoy His grace and mercy; *a stool,* where we may sit low at His feet and hear His blessed Word; *a candlestick,* from which the light of His testimony shines in a scene of darkness and doubt. Yes, Elisha had all of these, and our Lord has made that same simple provision for all of those who trust in Him.

These items were the emblem of the Shunammite woman's patronage of the man of God and all he represented. How beautifully the grace of Elisha shines in what directly ensued! Instead of being hurt at her scant hospitality, he called her to him one day and said: "Behold, thou hast been careful for us with *all this care.* What is to be done for thee? Wouldest thou be spoken for to the king or to the captain of the Lord's host?" She answered: *"I dwell among mine own people."* Thus her true attitude of heart was displayed. Her self-sufficiency had come to light. "I dwell among mine own people." What a reproof to Elisha's kindly grace!

She had all she wanted! She had her home, her friends, her own religion, her family and their good traditions, and she was quite content. *"I dwell among mine own people."*

OUR PATRONAGE

How graphically this illustrates the attitude of many nominal Christians towards the Lord Jesus; yes, an attitude in which perhaps all of us share in part! We have heard of Jesus, the Lord. His Gospel has come to our ears. The story of Bethlehem has long since entranced our childish hearts. Calvary's tale of sorrow and suffering has made a tear traverse our cheek. Then, in a kind of half-hearted way, we allowed the Lord Jesus to come into our life much as did the Shunammite woman bring Elisha into her home. We gave Jesus the outer chamber. With patronizing grace, mixed with a little human pride, He was assigned the guest-chamber, the spare room, lest sometimes we might be embarrassed before our friends if He were too much in evidence.

We would not want Him to go away altogether for there were those times when father was very sick, or one of the children was stricken, and the doctor spoke in a low whisper that struck like an arrow to our hearts. Then we invited Him in, and called Him "the great Physician" and asked Him to intercede. It gave us a feeling of security to know that He was close by, and so we furnished His outer chamber with scant care just so that He would not go away. After all, we did not need Him all the time. Most of the time we "dwell among our own people." We have our interests, our friends, our family, and like the proud lady, we only patronize the Man of God.

A VACANT HEART

"I dwell among mine own people" said the woman to Elisha, but the one to whom she spoke heard not her voice for he was looking into her heart. He knew there was a vacancy in her life that neither family nor friends would ever fill. She was childless and this was the echo of loneliness that pervaded her whole life. It had been the one long calamity of her life, and now she and her husband were older, and hope deferred had made her heart sick. Elisha, the prophet, told her to her utmost surprise that she would have a baby boy in her arms before the year ran out.

The boy was born to her in due time, and it seemed as though her life was full. Her self-satisfied life hitherto must have seemed empty and barren compared to the joy and content that flooded her home now. She had her heart's desire. Her home became brighter, and the sound of childish laughter and singing was heard in her villa. Yet still Elisha was only a tolerated guest who lived between journeys in the outer chamber under the roof of her patronage.

Then, when domestic happiness was at its height and it seemed the lady's heart was filled with joy, the little lad fell sick and died. Elisha was away then; he had gone on a journey. He *would* go on a journey just at a time when he was most needed! Oh, how she wished he were there then! She would give him the run of the house without question. She needed him so much! All her proud reserve was gone now. She was no longer the patron. She was a woman stricken with grief and anguish, and only Elisha could help. She threw her dignity to the winds and called for a young man to saddle an ass. He was too long in coming. She saddled it herself while she awaited his arrival, then said to him: "Drive; go forward; slack not thy riding for me except I bid thee."

The equipage set off across the hills, driving in desperate haste to reach Elisha. She found him not in the valley, nor at Shunem, for he had gone to Mount Carmel, that illustrious hill where Elijah, his master, had made the spectacular display of divine power in the fire that consumed the sacrifice. There she found Elisha.

THE SERVANT'S STAFF

When Elisha heard the lady's story of anguish, he told his servant, Gehazi, to take his staff and make all haste to her home, and lay it on the child. But it was of no avail. The servant's staff, typical of the law of Moses, will never bring life to one already dead.

Then Elisha went himself. He laid himself prostrate upon the child, his mouth to the child's mouth; his eyes to the child's eyes; his hands to the child's hands. Thus he completely identified himself with the little lad in the place of death, and presently new life coursed through the inert body of the child and he was restored to his astonished mother. Her heart was ravished, her spirit overwhelmed, and she cast herself in complete self-abasement at the feet of Elisha. Thus her patronage had been transformed to worship. Instead of showing measured and patronizing kindness to the man of God, she was found at his feet, owning him as her lord forever!

PATRONAGE CHANGED TO WORSHIP

Oh that this simple tale of grace and power might touch our hearts! If we have hitherto treated our Lord much as the Shunammite woman treated Elisha, assigning Him to the guest chamber at a convenient distance in our lives and homes, may we realize, as did this woman, that He is more than a man, a passing stranger! He is our Lord. In His hand are our destinies. He can give us the deepest desire of our hearts, and He can take it away, and He often does, but it is that we might no longer set our whole hearts upon things in this world. It is that He, Himself, might be our Lord; in our hearts, in our homes, in every sphere of our lives, that "in all things He might have the preeminence."

If we are only patrons of Christianity, going to church because it is the respectacle thing to do, and perhaps giving of our money to the Lord's work as a patron gives to a worthy cause, as though He needed our help, we miss the joy of the Lord and participate only in a religion.

Like the Shunammite woman, we must learn that the Lord Jesus alone can touch our dead hearts; that He has so completely identified Himself with us in death on Calvary's Cross, that now we live through Him, then and then alone can we call ourselves Christian.

May we cease to be patrons of a good cause and become worshippers, bowed low in the dust of repentance and the rapture of adoration before God's Man, the Life Giver to poor helpless sinners, the glorified Christ on heaven's throne today!

Chapter VII

FIGHTING OR FEASTING

In following the career of Elisha, the prophet, we have seen him lend a hand to a destitute widow, and change "a great woman" into a worshipper, and an earnest seeker after God.

IDLE PROPHETS

Elisha had been to Mount Carmel, the place of sacrifice. At the Shunammite woman's behest, he had come down and brought her child back to life. As the next episode unfolds, he is making his way with his servant down to the town of Gilgal close by. This, fittingly enough, seems to have been somewhat of a religious center. It was the town where one in those days might see the stones that had been set up as memorials to celebrate the triumph of the crossing of the Jordan by God's ancient people. It had become a fair haven for the Lord's prophets to assemble and, overcome by the apathy of the times, they seemed to have lapsed into a kind of indifference that so often besets the Lord's servants in idleness. Idleness always pays large dividends, but they are the dividends of dearth and famine. (2 Kings 4:38-44.)

"DEATH IN THE POT"

When Elisha came among them, he found these young prophets idly wondering what might happen next. A dearth had spread through the land, and they were evidently too dignified to bestir themselves to seek a remedy. But Elisha was a man of action, as is every true man of God. He saw his brethren sitting indolently in their apathetic dignity; he roused them to action at once, and sent them out to the adjoining neighborhood to gather herbs while he put a pot on the fire to bring it to boil. He was going to give them a meal such as they had not had in months, for indolent inactivity always leads to want and starvation.

Encouraged by such a valiant leader, the young prophets seem to have gone out with a will, but one of them had more enthusiasm than wisdom. He came upon a luscious vine that hung in a sequestered nook of the valley, laden with large fruits such as he had never seen before. He gathered them hastily, not knowing that they were poisonous gourds. He brought them into camp and, in his diligence, put them into the pot which was already seething upon the fire, mingling his poisonous gourds with the rich and delicious herbs that made the pottage.

Evidently he was unnoticed by his brethren, for soon the meal was ready and Elisha spread it before them. But a hue and cry soon went up from the hungry diners for they detected a strange flavor and they shouted, "There's death in the pot!"

A HANDFUL OF MEAL

Had Elisha been either a seeker for self-prominence, or a religious dreamer, he would have made every effort to discover the culprit who had poisoned the food, that he might be duly punished for his offense. But the hunger of his brethren was more to Elisha than the detection of the criminal. He did a strange thing. He took a handful of meal. He put it into the pot. The good meal counteracted the poison. The pottage was sweet and good. His religious compatriots then enjoyed the food to the full, and the culprit was perhaps one of these whose hunger was assuaged by the pottage which he unwittingly had spoiled.

SPIRITUAL APATHY

In all of this we have a wonderfully vivid picture of that which has a very real counterpart in our day and age. We who profess to be the Lord's people in this present day have reached a stage of dignified apathy which words cannot describe. There was a time in the history of the church when the followers of Christ accepted with zeal the reproach and scorn of the world. As time rolled on, and the religious world became a flourishing enterprise which named the Name of Christ but denied the power of that Name, we have sought to make ourselves popular in it. Serving the Lord has become a popular profession, and a mark of dignity instead of a lonely road of reproach such as the Apostle Paul and Simon Peter knew in their day.

Like these prophets in Gilgal, the Lord's people have sat down amid the shrines of our traditional faith, extolling the past and lapsing into a state of inertia that the Scripture calls "lukewarmness." With our inactivity has come a great dearth and, instead of being men fired with a zeal for God, enriched in our own spirits with the grace of Christ and the knowledge of our Lord, we have become emaciated spiritually, until we find ourselves in a land of famine, and we need an Elisha.

RELIGIOUS GOURDS

Usually the man of God on such an occasion comes from a most unexpected quarter, and his voice re-echoes alarm through the land. It is then that the true distinction between the real servants of the Lord and those who are without knowledge is seen. The false and the real go out together, and they gather herbs, and with their ingathering come the useless gourds of speculative religion. It is all put into a pot together and a great mixture of religious pottage is set down before the hungry. The cry then goes up that "there is death in the pot." But instead of being concerned about the hungry and the dying, we go in search of the culprits.

So-called champions of the faith shout from the housetops of their own citadels of religious beliefs until the whole camp is divided against itself into opposing parties. Each calls the other the poison monger and, while they each fire broadside salvos from their own proud embattlements at each other, the famine goes on and the multitudes have nothing to feed their hungry hearts.

PASTORAL CARE

How we need men like Elisha to step forth and put a handful of genuine "meal" in the pot as an antidote to the nauseous gourds of man's religion! How good it would be in this day and age if we had men like Elisha in greater numbers who, instead of spending their religious energy in fighting their brethren far and near, would put a little "meal in the pot." In other words, if they would only bring the true bread of God to feed the people. The bread of God is Christ who alone can feed the hungry and counteract the poison of man's foolish religion.

Our Lord Himself has said: "I am the bread of life. He that cometh to Me shall never hunger, and he that believeth on Me shall never thirst."

How sad it is that we have so many religious champions today and so few real pastors and shepherds! Men want bread and we give them a stone. We are organizing nationally into groups to fight each other when men are dying without Christ and the flock of God goes hungry. We have laid aside the shepherd's staff and we have taken up the sword. The green pastures have been turned into a religious battlefield where moral and spiritual conflict rages amid the scenes of famine. That is the lesson that comes home with tragic realism in this story of Elisha and the hungry prophets in 2 Kings 4. We need only to put "meal in the pot." The meal offering in Israel's day spoke of Christ in His sinless perfection of manhood. Such ministry alone can feed the souls of men in days of famine.

BREAD ENOUGH AND TO SPARE

Then notice how this wonderful episode closes. No sooner had Elisha set this wholesome food before the sons of the prophets than a stranger came from the region beyond, carrying with him not the scanty pickings of herbs from the wayside, but a rich supply of bread of the first-fruits, twenty loaves of barley and full ears of corn. We may be sure that, if we use the food which God gives to us in the day of famine, and seek to minister it to others, He will then send us a more abundant supply.

Now that the prophets were fed from the scanty store of their own gathering, the meal mingled with it, this stranger came up from the country with bread enough and to spare. The vast multitude of the people themselves were then set down. Elisha took the food, set it before them, and it was enlarged by God Himself, much as our Saviour enlarged the store of the five loaves and the two fishes on the lakeside of Galilee, so that they were all filled and satisfied, and there was plenty left over.

Let us then humbly seek to bring Christ to the world, to realize that the hearts of men are empty, that their souls are starving, and there is a dearth in the land. Let us remember well that the Gospel is still the power of God unto salvation to every one that believeth; that Christ is the only Saviour, and that we who profess His name have the only food for the soul, the only panacea for man's cruel sorrows and afflictions, and the bread of life for all mankind.

Chapter VIII

NAAMAN — THE LEPER

Among the many interesting episodes in the life of Elisha, the prophet, none is more familiar to us than the story of Naaman, the leper. This is perhaps one of the most picturesque illustrations of the simple truth of the gospel of God's grace to be found in the entire Bible. No one, having read the story, could fail to understand God's way of salvation. The setting is most interesting.

DAYS OF ADVERSITY

Those were days of adversity for God's people, Israel. Their idolatry and God-forgetfulness had led them into paths of dishonor and great national weakness. Their traditional enemies, the Syrians, had made inroads upon them and had, on one occasion, carried away captive a little girl who remains nameless in God's inspired Book. Strangely enough this Israelite maid, now a slave in a strange land, found herself in the home of the great Syrian general called Naaman. She was destined to bear a bright testimony there to the faith of her fathers.

A GREAT MAN — BUT A LEPER

In 2 Kings 5, Naaman is described in brilliant letters of the highest commendation. He was evidently the highest military man in the land, held in great esteem by his master, the King of Syria. Unlike the somewhat typical soldier, there was nothing swashbuckling and overbearing about this man. On the contrary, the Scripture describes him as being "honorable," or, more accurately, the Hebrew word means "gracious." Moreover, he was a man of outstanding courage, and evidently did ample credit to his rank and station both in act and in demeanor. As far as his fellows were concerned, every head in the land looked up to Naaman. A man of brilliant achievement, of unquestioned honor, of popular appeal, of gracious behavior, there seemed nothing wanting in this illustrious personality. Having commended Naaman with unqualified praise, however, the Scripture appends to the catalogue of his goodness one stark and tragic fact about this man which beclouds all the others — "But he was a leper."

A LITTLE GIRL'S FAITH

One can well imagine that this gallant soldier managed to keep secret the foul blot that besmirched his person, and for a long time it may have proved little hindrance in his career as a national hero. But there was one sphere in which he moved where it was well known. That was in his home. Among the retinue of servants who were privileged to serve in his household it was the whispered secret, and when it reached the ears of the maid of Israel who was captive in his home she exclaimed: "Would God my lord were with the prophet that is in Samaria, for he would recover him of his leprosy!" Mark the confidence of this girl who knew well the power of Elisha's God.

The report of the faith in this maiden reached the ears of Naaman and he took immediate action. He went to the Syrian King. He secured letters of introduction to the King of Israel whose land he had vanquished. He gathered together a suitable offering that he might carry it with due fanfare and pompous display as a token of his prominence and worthiness to receive the cleansing to be had in Israel's land. But he met with disappointment. The King of Israel was abashed at the very idea that one should think of him as God, to kill or to make alive, and he feared that this gallant general had come back to ensnare him into a renewal of conflict between the warlike Syrians and his own nation.

A PROPHET IN ISRAEL

Elisha, the true man of God, ever characteristically in the background, heard of the plight of Israel's king and indicated that the man Naaman should be sent to him that he might learn once and for all that there was a prophet in Israel. So one day there came along the highway a magnificent caravan of military grandeur which unexpectedly stopped outside the door of the prophet's dwelling. Naaman must have been exceedingly surprised when the prophet did not even come to the door to greet him. Instead, Elisha sent one of his messengers with the simple instructions: "Go and wash in Jordan seven times, and thy flesh shall come again to thee, and thou shalt be clean."

HIS HUMILIATION

Naaman was very angry. He had expected that the man of God would come with great ceremony to him and strike his hand over the leprous spot, calling dramatically on the Name of his God. Dipping in a muddy river might be all very well for a common soldier in the ranks of his army, but there should be a more ceremonious method for a four-star general. "Go and wash seven times in Jordan," that river which was so unattractive compared to the crystal streams of Damascus! It could not be!

But Naaman's friends who had traveled with him so far that he might be recovered from his leprosy, pleaded with him to sink his pride, to overcome his feeling of humiliation, and obey the simple command of God's prophet. Their solicitation prevailed upon him, and the caravan wended its way down to the murky stream called Jordan.

One can envision the gallant soldier arriving at Jordan's banks, his uniform beribboned in token of many a victorious campaign, his military bearing bespeaking so much dignity and courage, yet everyone knowing that beneath his panoplied grandeur there was that foul and loathsome disease for which there was no remedy. That is to say, no remedy except this new, untried cure, "Go and wash seven times in Jordan."

ONLY A LEPER

The dignified soldier descended from his chariot, the warlike steeds champing at the bit as he alighted. What a picture he must have presented of offended dignity, of honor in humiliation! He divested himself of the uniform that bespoke his rank and covered the secret of his disease. Then stripped of his dignity, his honor, his rank, and even his pride, he stood for a moment on Jordan's banks, now nothing more than a man—yes, a man who was a leper. Then down into the murky stream he went.

What questions must have knocked upon the door of his heart! What misgivings must have torn his spirit as he wondered what foolhardy system of cleansing this could be that was devised by Elisha! But he who has a hopeless disease will do much for its relief. "All that a man hath will he give for his life."

SEVEN TIMES IN JORDAN

Naaman decided to try this strangest remedy that had ever come to his ears. Down he went into the water and washed once, twice, three times; probably pausing in between to see if there was any improvement on that tell-tale patch of whiteness upon his skin. But it was still as vile and livid as ever. Four times, five times, six times! His eager gaze fell upon the leprous spot, but it was still leprous. Would the absurd humiliating process never end? The man of God had said "seven times," and for the seventh time Naaman washed again in the muddy waters of Jordan's river. As he finished, what miracle was this that had been wrought? His flesh was like that of a little child. The leprosy was gone and he stood clean and whole. The man of God was right. The loathsome disease had vanished.

As Naaman came up from the river bed, he was a new man, regenerated, born anew, with a new lease on a new life. The sadness which had been his constant companion ever since he had first seen the earliest indication of the dread disease upon his body had left him now. Joy and gladness filled his heart. His first impulse was to reward Elisha for his goodness, but the man of God sought no reward, nor would be take any. Elisha had been God's messenger of grace and kindness, not to Naaman the proud general, but to Naaman the leper. No paltry gift from the hand of a leper could ever pay for his cleansing.

CLEANSED FROM OUR SINS

It is not difficult to see in this wonderful story of the cleansing of Naaman the gospel of God's matchless grace toward us all. Leprosy, the dread disease, is the tragic type of sin's dark stain which is upon every son of Adam's fallen race. Like Naaman, we also may have a long catalogue of fine accomplishments, of courageous exploits. We may ride high in honorable dignity and conduct ourselves among our fellows with gracious demeanor and amiable acceptability. We may stand well in the graces and esteem of the elite of the land, but underneath the panoply of our courage, beneath the proud vestments of honor and respectability among our fellows, there is a stain of sin upon us all. We may hide its cruel ravages from the social circle in which we move. Our friends in business may know little of its power in our lives, but in our homes it is known as was Naaman's.

ALL HAVE SINNED

In that intimate circle where we are best known, where the flimsy covering of our honor and grace means little, the dark secret passes from lip to lip. Here in the inner sanctuary of our home life it is an open secret, and it is fortunate indeed if, like Naaman, we have some humble person much like Israel's captive maid, to tell us about the prophet of Samaria. His Name is Jesus, the Lord, who can heal us of our leprosy. Then, having heard the good news, how good to have the wisdom of Naaman to find our way into the presence of God's prophet; to listen to His word: "The blood of Jesus Christ, God's Son, cleanses us from all sin."

THE ONLY REMEDY

For a man of high rank like Naaman, it must have seemed a very undignified way of obtaining cleansing to wash seven times in Jordan. It may seem very undignified for us who are spiritual lepers to hear the news that we must be cleansed by the blood of Christ. No use bringing a gift; it is unacceptable; it will not bring cleansing! No use getting angry as did Naaman because of the simplicity of the way! There is nothing we can do, nothing we can bring that will remove the foul stain of sin from our person. "There is none other name under heaven, given among men whereby we must be saved." Neither our fine character nor our good deeds will bring about cleansing from sin. Only the blood of Christ can do that. We must accept Christ as Saviour, and His blood shed as our atonement. "Purge me with hyssop," said the psalmist, "and I shall be clean; wash me, and I shall be whiter than snow."

Chapter IX

THE AX HEAD SWIMS

It is not surprising that in the colorful life of the prophet, Elisha, there are so many exquisitely simple yet beautiful illustrations of the gospel of God's grace. Elisha was characteristically the man of grace, wending his way across the landscape in his day much as our Lord Himself traveled much later along the roads of Judea and Samaria, entering into the homespun simplicity of the life of the people. Thus there is an endearing similarity between the conduct of Elisha in the opening chapters of the Second Book of Kings, and that of our Saviour as found in the four Gospels of the New Testament.

We have seen Elisha, much like our Lord Himself, relieve the calamitous bankruptcy of a poor widow, and raise a little child from the dead to gladden the heart of its mother, changing her from a proud, self-sufficient woman to a worshipper who loved him much. We have seen him, too, by miraculous power bring cleansing to a leprous soldier called Naaman, and bring him also into the spirit of humble gratitude.

THE WAY TOO NARROW

In 2 Kings 6, Elisha is found among the young prophets who had come to dwell with him, no doubt to learn something of the grace and wisdom which he manifested so much in his life. As disciples and pupils of this man of God, they soon found, as many young prophets do, that Elisha's manner of life was too restricted for them, and that following in his footsteps became increasingly difficult. They soon came to the conclusion that his dwelling was not quite large enough to give scope to their young ambitions and their liberal ideas. They went to him with the confession: "Behold now the place where we dwell with thee is too straight for us. Let us go, we pray thee, unto Jordan, and take thence every man a beam, and let us make a place where we may dwell."

Elisha, being a wise man, did not seek to curb their ambition, for he knew that bondage never brings a person into the line of the will of the Lord. He let them have their way, therefore, and very soon the sound of the axe re-echoed among the trees of the forest hard by Jordan's banks. There must have been exultant relief in the hearts of the young prophets, who had sat so long under the tutelage of this faithful man of God, as they were suddenly released from their devotions. They went into the woods, swinging their axes with a will. The simplicities of life with Elisha were to be exchanged for a more liberal existence. The humble dwelling where they had been domiciled with Elisha was to be exchanged for a more ambitious and more elegant edifice. The simple meeting house was to be abandoned and a new cathedral built. They evidently appreciated Elisha's godliness, but he was a man of ideas that were too restricted and too small for them, and they were going in for bigger things!

BIG THINGS ARE SMALL

It is interesting to see that Elisha did not stand in their way, for no doubt he knew the futility of it. He knew, too, that God has a way of teaching His followers the smallness of those things which men call "big." His thoughts may have been re-echoed by Paul in the New Testament: "God hath chosen the foolish things of the world to confound the wise . . . , the weak things of the world to confound the things which are mighty, and base things of the world, and things which are despised hath God chosen, yea, and things which are not, to bring to naught things that are. That no flesh should glory in his presence." (1 Cor. 1: 27-29.) But the young prophets had other ideas. They would erect a building more in keeping with their young ambitions, wherein they could live in a style suitable to the dignity of their calling.

THE AX HEAD FALLS

So the axes were swung in the forest, and the trees were felled. One young man, no doubt one of the poorer prophets, had to borrow an ax. He swung it lustily, indeed a little too lustily, and as it made a glancing blow on the tree trunk, the ax head came off, shooting straight as an arrow for the river Jordan into which it fell and sank to the bottom. This must have been most humiliating to a young and somewhat dignified prophet.

A borrowed ax had been lost and where would he find means of restitution to the owner? In his plight, he went to Elisha and the man of grace, instead of taking the attitude of "I told you so," or driving home the folly of his over-zealous action, inquired of the young man as to where the ax had sunk. The young prophet pointed to the spot. Then Elisha reached up and broke a live branch from a tree which overhung the river. He cast the live branch into the murky stream and, to the consternation of the young man, the iron ax head came to the surface, swimming like a living thing. He picked it up at the word of Elisha and all was well!

THE MODERN TEMPO

In this picturesque circumstance in the career of Elisha, the prophet, there is a magnificent illustration of the gospel of God's grace. It is the ageless story, old, yet ever new, that the Father sent the Son to be the Saviour of the world. The days recounted in 2 Kings 6 are much like our own modern times. We are in the midst of a scene where we are hearing the words of the young prophets re-echo through the land. The boundaries set upon our life by the antitype of Elisha, who is none other than the Lord Jesus Himself, are too narrow for our modern ideas. Their restrictions are irksome to the young aspirants of modern philosophy. The limitations placed upon our lives by that godliness which was taught by the Lord Jesus Himself might be good enough for simple fishermen like Simon Peter and James and John, but the doctrine of the day is to trim our sails to the wind. We must suit Christianity to the modern tempo! We must change with the times! The simple meeting house of the upper room for the early disciples of our Lord must be supplanted by the grand cathedral, the white-robed choir and resonant pipe organ.

OUT-MODED SIMPLICITIES

In the days recorded in the Acts of the Apostles godly women like Lydia and her companions might meet under the azure blue of heaven by the river-side to hold their simple prayer meeting, but things are different now! We must make the prayer meeting more attractive to the masses, and season the occasion with adequate entertainment! These are but the echoes of the voices of the young prophets in the days of Elisha. There is no use standing in its way for the spirit of the age is for grander and bigger things. The quiet simplicities of godliness do not suit the hour.

BORROWED POWER

Religion has become big business, featuring big men and much ostentation, but, while they are cutting beams for bigger and better houses of worship and grander dwelling places, let us remember the story of the ax head. Let us remember that the power by which we build is *borrowed* power. Whatever talents we may be using to fashion the trees of the forest into beams for our new and more elegant structure of life have been given to us by the Lord, who will demand an account of the way in which we use those talents. Let us remember also, that our ambitious operations are going forward on the very banks of Jordan, for the waters of death roll close by for every one of us. We must learn, too, the lesson of the live branch plucked from the growing tree and cast into Jordan's water that the ax head might swim.

THE LORD MUST BUILD

What a wonderful picture of Christ, our Saviour, who once looked down upon the wayward ways of men here in this world and saw the futility of all their efforts, knowing that "except the Lord build the house, they labor in vain that build it." The power by which we build for self-aggrandizement is destined to fall out of our control into the dark stream of death itself, there to sink in the waters of judgment and write the final doom to all our proud ambitions. But knowing all of this, God Himself in His matchless grace has taken the live branch from the growing tree of life, a beautiful type of our Lord and Saviour.

THE LIVING BRANCH

The Living One left those heights of matchless glory where "He thought it not robbery to be equal with God, but made himself of no reputation, and took upon him the form of a servant, and was made in the likeness of men. And being found in fashion as a man, He humbled himself and became obedient unto death, even the death of the cross." The live branch went down into Jordan's waters! The Living One became dead! The One who is eternal, who ever dwells in the Father's affection, came down here into this world of woe, and on the Cross of Calvary died the death of shame and degradation as the sin bearer. He, the Living Branch, went into the waters of death and we hear His cry: "Save me, oh God, for the waters are come in unto my soul. I sink in deep mire, where there is no standing, I am come into deep waters where the floods overflow me . . . Deliver me out of the mire and let me not sink. Let not the waterflood overflow me, neither let the deep swallow me up and let not the pit shut her mouth upon me." (Psa. 69: 1, 2, 14, 15.)

HE DIED THAT WE MIGHT LIVE

These were prophetically the utterances of our Lord, the Messiah, as He went down into "Jordan's stream" in order that we who had sunk down under the power of death might be raised up from the pit and the miry clay, and our feet set upon the rock. What it meant to the eternal Son of God to go into death no human heart will ever know. "He who knew no sin became sin for us that we might become God's righteousness in Him." He sank down under the waters in order that we might be saved; He died that we might live.

But He was also "the Living Branch," and He rose from the dead. In resurrection life He is building His church, "and the gates of hell shall not prevail against it." (Matt. 16:18.)

Chapter X

OPEN THE YOUNG MAN'S EYES

In 2 Kings 6, Israel's inveterate enemy, the king of Syria, had planned by wicked stealth to destroy them, but Elisha, God's prophet, forewarned Israel's king of the evil devices of his adversary so that the nation was delivered. Then Elisha seemed to retire into the obscurity of one of those many seasons of quiet communion with his God that so often intervened between the higher lights of his public testimony. The king of Syria, baffled at the mysterious frustration of his well laid plans, sent spies to discover Elisha. They found him in Dothan, and that is quite striking.

It calls to memory at once Joseph, that beloved servant of God of many years before. When he was a young lad of seventeen, Joseph was sent by his father to search out his brethren, and in his lonely quest after their welfare, he found them at long last in Dothan. It was there that they so cruelly abused him, and sold him as a slave to the Midianites. Perhaps Elisha and his servant, as they rested among the quiet verdant hills in the little city of Dothan, remembered that this town had been made famous because of Joseph and his brethren.

ELISHA PRAYED

Early one morning, as the golden sunlight splashed its rosy hues across the eastern horizon beyond the hills, Elisha's servant stepped forth from the threshold of their humble dwelling to find to his astonishment that the city was surrounded by a host of Syrian warriors determined upon the destruction of himself and his master. He ran to Elisha and said, "Alas, my master, how shall we do?" Then his master, with that easy grace and calm courage that has ever characterized the true servants of God, answered the trembling young man in these magnificent words: "Fear not, for they that be with us are more than they that be with them."

A look of incredulous astonishment must have come upon the face of the young man as he heard these strange words from the lips of his master. As far as the eye could see around the city, there was an armed host of belligerent enemies with no sign of a friend anywhere. "Fear not," said Elisha, "they that be with us are more than they that be with them." But words alone were small consolation before the impelling force of the sight of all those enemies, and Elisha was not unsympathetic for the fear and dread that possessed his beloved follower.

Then the Scripture says so beautifully: "Elisha prayed." He did not pray for deliverance from his enemies because he knew that was sure. His prayer was on behalf of the young man, that the Lord would find a ready means of centering his confidence upon Jehovah. Elisha said, "Lord I pray thee, open his eyes that he may see." And the Lord opened the eyes of the young man and he saw: "and, behold, the mountain was full of horses and chariots of fire round about Elisha."

"FEAR NOT"

In this wonderfully dramatic episode we have a scene which sets forth in colors of great grandeur some of the most encouraging truths for Christian hearts today. The Devil, our arch enemy, has gathered together his forces of belligerent power and they surround the Christian camp at this very hour to make assault upon our faith. We are living in the last days when Satan is making one grand assault, not only upon the citadel of Christian truth, but upon the people of God themselves, in order that he might destroy finally and completely every vestige of testimony for Christ from off the earth. He has managed to create confusion and chaos in the world at large; the cruel scourge of war's fear is laid across the backs of the nations; international tension is near the breaking point, but Satan's one great desire, which overtops everything else, is that he might destroy all Christian testimony. These are the days in which we find ourselves. We look abroad across the spiritual landscape and we see our "city of Dothan," the city of Joseph and his brethren, of Elisha and his servant, of Christ and His people, surrounded on every hand by the forces of Satan, ready to do battle against us, and much like Elisha's servant, we tremble in our shoes at the very sight.

Yet we also have an "Elisha" to whom we can go. The Elisha of today sits on the throne of God on high, and as we come to Him, trembling and in fear sometimes, we hear His blessed words: "Fear not, for they that be with us are more than they that be with them."

In the words of our Lord and Saviour it is this: "In the world ye shall have tribulation, but be of good cheer, I have overcome the world." "What shall we say then to these things; if God be for us, who can be against us?" And "Greater is he that is in you, than he that is in the world."

He who sits on heaven's throne at this hour tells us in tones of deepest affection as His voice comes to us through the shadows: "Peace I leave with you; my peace I give unto you; not as the world giveth, give I unto you, let not your heart be troubled, neither let it be afraid." And, "Lo, I am with you always, even unto the end of the age."

These are but the living echoes of Elisha's words to his servant in the town of Dothan: "Fear not, for they that be with us are more than they that be with them." Not only did Elisha speak the reassuring word, but he retired into his chamber, and kneeled before the Lord and prayed for the young man, asking the Lord to open his eyes. How similar this is to the present session of our Lord Himself, our Great High Priest, who has gone into the peace and quiet of those celestial regions where "He ever liveth to make intercession for us."

OUR GREAT HIGH PRIEST

There was an occasion in the life of the Lord's beloved disciple, Simon Peter, when the Devil and his legions surrounded him that they might make a grand assault upon the citadel of his faith, just as the host of Syrians surrounded the town where Elisha and his servant lived. But the Lord said to Simon: "Satan hath desired to have you that he may sift you as wheat; but I have prayed for thee that thy faith fail not; and when thou are restored, strengthen thy brethren." (Luke 22: 31, 32.)

How the Devil must have laughed with complacent and evil delight when he heard poor Simon Peter deny his Lord with oaths and curses! The battle was going against Simon Peter that night as he sat in the courtyard at the high priest's house and told them, with ugly and most unseemly language, that he never knew the Man called Jesus. It seemed a great triumph for Satan to have this trembling disciple disown his Lord, but Jesus had prayed for him and the time came when the restored Simon Peter stood valiantly forth on the day of Pentecost, and it was his turn then to make a grand assault upon the citadel of Satan's domain.

In Acts 2, Simon Peter stood up fearlessly amid the thousands who had flocked to the city of Jerusalem that they might hear the tidings of this One called Jesus who had died and had risen from the dead. Then Simon Peter gathered together all the armaments of the power of the Spirit of God, and discharged a broadside salvo upon the forces of wickedness, making such an inroad upon their battlements that he carried away three thousand prisoners into the camp of the Lord on that one day. The Devil's temporary victory was turned into cruel defeat and disorderly retreat, and Simon, the faltering, failing disciple who had denied his Lord, stood upon the field of battle with three thousand new converts gathered around him as a witness that has shone like the noonday sun down through the centuries. "They that be with us are more than they that be with them."

ROUND ABOUT ELISHA

The priestly service of our Lord is still available to us in the present time but we do not properly estimate its value. Jesus the Christ, the Son of God has risen from the dead, the mighty Victor. All who stand by His side, even as the servant stood by Elisha's side, will be victorious. Elisha prayed for his servant. Jesus the Lord prayed for Simon Peter, and our Lord and Saviour, seated at the right hand of God on high, is praying for us. Not that we might be saved from defeat, because in Him we are already victorious. His prayer, like that of Elisha, is: "Open his eyes, that he may see."

When the young man's eyes were opened, he looked abroad. His vision had been short and blurred before, so that he was unable to see beyond the heads of the host that surrounded the city in which he stood, but now he looked beyond with divine perception, to the hills that skirted the whole valley, and he saw them alive with horses and chariots of fire, round about Elisha.

Notice that expression: "Round about Elisha." As long as the young man stayed close to Elisha there could be no question of his safety, for that armed host of divine might found its center in Elisha himself. The young man's place of safety was by the side of his master, even as our place of safety is by the side of Christ, our Lord.

Let us look beyond the murky fog that enswathes the earth about us, being less occupied with the Devil's prowess as he makes his assault upon us from every hand in the world today, and let us look to the empyrean hills of heaven itself and see the celestial heights, peopled with a vast army of divine might, and say with God-given confidence: "If God be for us, who can be against us?"

Chapter XI

FAMINE IN SAMARIA

One of the most dramatic stories in all the Bible is found in 2 Kings 6 and 7. There were many crises in the time of Elisha, but surely this was the greatest of them all, and we cannot read the impelling drama without seeing how many of its details find a distinct parallel in our own critical modern life.

For a while the Syrians, those inveterate enemies of Elisha's people, had laid aside their warlike habits and the land had rested quietly under the glad sunshine of peace. But now the belligerent Syrians again bestirred themselves among the hills and descended once more to lay prolonged and embattled siege against Samaria where Elisha's people dwelt.

Days and months rolled on, but there was no egress from the city to the fertile country beyond, and grievous famine took hold of the people. They were reduced to such awful conditions that the very refuse of the streets was scraped together and sold at a high price for whatever sustenance it might afford the human skeletons who roamed the city. The beasts of burden were slaughtered for food, sold at famine prices, and even a donkey's head, nothing but skin and bone, brought the equivalent of forty-five dollars.

A FAMINE STRICKEN CITY

Indeed so grievously did the famine lay its black scourge upon the city of Samaria that two women made a bargain with each other as to that fateful day on which they would boil their children for food, and even fought over their broken contract when their hearts rebelled at carrying out such an agreement. Even the king in the royal palace, high on the wall of the city, would be seen ambulating upon the parapet wearing sackcloth beneath his royal garments, proclaiming to all that he shared the sorrows of his people.

God's prophet Elisha, the man of grace, had quite recently shown some beneficent kindness to the Syrians who now besieged the gates, and his own people in the city now attributed the siege to his pious folly, laying the blame for their cruel plight at the feet of Elisha.

ELISHA'S STARTLING PREDICTION

True to the dignity of his calling however, Elisha replied to their false accusations by making a most startling announcement. It was a dramatic moment. The royal decree had gone forth that Elisha's head should come off, and the executioner was on his way to the humble dwelling where Elisha and his brethren sat within, in contrite mourning before the Lord. When the executioner arrived at Elisha's door, the prophet instructed his brethren to hold him fast that he might listen to the announcement of grace that would fall from Elisha's lips. Then these words fell upon the skeptical ears of the executioner. "Tomorrow about this time, a measure of fine flour shall be sold for a shekel, and two measures of barley for a shekel in the gate of Samaria."

The announcement was greeted with scoffing unbelief on every hand, for how could a famished people believe that an army could be dispersed and provisions brought from afar within twenty-four hours? Human logic shouted: "If God made windows in heaven how could this thing be?" But man's extremity has always been God's opportunity, and God did not need to pour grain in an avalanche from the sky to fulfill His Word, for the Lord has His own way of baffling human reasoning and laying our hearts in adoring wonder and worship before Him.

FOUR LEPROUS MEN

Among the many despondent inhabitants of the famine ridden city of Samaria were four leprous men, who sat huddled together in the isolation of their double calamity of hunger and disease. Their plight was surely the most desperate of all in that city, and the most hopeless. They had no human vigor or robust manhood upon which they could rely, and they knew that they stood between two fires of desperation, famine and disease. In their extremity, however, they decided to do something about it.

They argued with themselves that if they sat still in the besieged city they would die anyway, so why not go out into the camp of the enemy, for peradventure they might find food there. Of course they might be killed at the hand of the enemy, but apparently they were going to die anyway, so why not take a chance?

For months the host of armed warriors had entrenched themselves like a ring of steel about the city, but in the gathering dusk of the twilight that evening, these four desperate men could be seen furtively pursuing their way through the streets and lanes of the city toward the outskirts. As the darkness fell across the landscape, they pursued their foolhardy journey out to the besieged gate, stealthily found their way beyond the embattlements, and crept into the enemy camp.

A DESERTED CAMP

What must have been their consternation when, instead of hearing the expected challenge of the sentry, they heard not a sound? Out there in the darkness, they could dimly discern horses tethered at the tents and donkeys tied by their feeding troughs, but not a sound could they hear save the quiet rustle of the wind in the deserted camp. It was all as peaceful as a graveyard. Into one tent they went to find a table spread as if they had been expected guests, but no host was there to greet them or to repel them. They sat down to satisfy their aching hunger and rose from the table to find the tents filled with treasures of gold and silver which they hid away for future reference.

The truth was that the Lord Jehovah, by miraculous power, had caused a great rushing noise to come suddenly upon the ears of the Syrian warriors so that it sounded as if an armed host of overwhelming power and number was suddenly descending upon them. They had evidently been thus surprised as they sat down to their evening meal. They had left it untouched and had fled in terror without even taking time to mount their horses, leaving behind them food in abundance, and treasures of untold value. All of this was the sudden inheritance which the four leprous men had come upon so unexpectedly. They returned to the city in great glee, proclaiming the glad tidings of release and deliverance from famine. Accordingly, when morning dawned, a measure of fine flour was sold for a shekel, and two measures of barley for a shekel in the gate of Samaria.

Even as Elisha had said, the hour of terror was over. The embattled city was set free, the famine turned into a feast, the captives delivered, the scoffing unbelievers put to shame, and the Name of Jehovah exalted once more.

OUR FOES

The gospel of God's grace is graphically illustrated in this dramatic episode. The city of Samaria is but a picture of this present world that lies in the inexorable grip of the evil one. Satan, with his fell legions in all their spiritual power, stands in wicked array around us all. We are beset by foes without and within even as were these people in Elisha's day. The foe without is the Devil with all his evil forces that would ensnare us in the captive bonds of eternal ruin. The foe within is that which lies latent in the heart of every man and woman here in this world, sin and unbelief.

Like these Samaritans of old, we are all too apt to turn upon the Man of God who, like Elisha, has besprent our pathway with nothing but loving kindness and grace on every hand. How many people in the world still blame God and His Christ for the calamitous evils in which we find ourselves! Jesus, the Lord, God's Man, entered this world of woe in the humble fashion of manhood's grace, bringing to mankind far and near the love of a Father's heart. He died the cruel death of Calvary's Cross in order that men might come out of the darkness of their calamity into the marvelous light of His Kingdom. Yet men scoffed at His offers of mercy and cast Him out, and blamed Him for their sorrows.

OUR EXTREMITY

We sit today among the tangled debris of the folly of centuries, spiritual famine over-spreads the land, and the Devil himself and his armies of wicked power do their utmost to ensnare us to destruction. Yet some of us, like the four leprous men of Samaria, have sat down and taken counsel together, realizing the extremity of our condition, realizing that the hand of death is upon us, and we had better do something about it. "If we do nothing, we'll die," was their conclusion, and that may well be ours, too. All we need do in order to die eternally is *"nothing."*

"How shall we escape if we neglect so great salvation?" says the Scripture. "He that believeth not the Son shall not see life, but the wrath of God abideth on him." These are the stark realities that loom before our vision as sinners away from God, with the power of the Devil surrounding us. Oh, that we all had the wisdom of the four leprous men to bestir ourselves, to get upon our feet and make diligent search for a place of safety. The only place of safety is in the Devil's abandoned camp, a place called Calvary.

THE MIGHTY VICTOR

On Golgatha's dark hill, two thousand years ago, the fell

legions of Satan's mighty power gathered themselves together in black, imposing array against the Son of God that they might do battle to the finish against Him who took our place and undertook to be our Deliverer. On that dark night that enshrouded this fair creation, when the noonday sun should have flooded the scene in kindly brilliance with light and life, there was enacted a battle between the lonely Son of the living God, and all Satan's power. Every evil device that hell could devise was brought into play. All the Devil's wicked legions, with their every last reserve, were brought to the front, and men energized by their own folly under Satan's might, ranged themselves like a ring of steel about the Person of God's Son for His destruction.

In Elisha's day, the Syrian host outside Samaria heard a noise at the most unexpected moment, at the very hour when their triumph seemed secure, at supper time when the feast of victory was spread. As the enemy was about to celebrate the laurels of his triumph, a thunderous rushing noice, God's voice, was heard.

THE TRIUMPH AT CALVARY

On Calvary's rugged hill, when the shades of night had fallen and the noonday sun had shrunk behind the clouds, Satan with his host of demons and his army of wicked men, was about to celebrate the final victory over the Son of God. Then a voice was heard, and it was the voice of thunder. The universe was shaken to its very core; creation's vault re-echoed with the mighty shout. It came, not from heaven with flashing fire or terror-laden crash, but from the parched lips of the lowly Son of Man who hung on the Tree, declaring in a loud voice that shook heaven, earth and hell: *"It is finished."*

If we are going to find deliverance, we must find it at Calvary, for there Satan was defeated, his camp abandoned, and his hosts put to flight. There today we find the peace unspeakable of death conquered, sin put away, the Devil annulled.

Now a measure of fine flour may be sold for a shekel, and two measures of barley for a shekel. We may have Christ as Saviour for our eternal redemption. "Ho, everyone that thirsteth, come ye to the waters, and he that hath no money, come ye buy and eat, yea come, buy wine and milk, without money and without price."

"For the same Lord over all is rich unto all that call upon Him, and whoever shall call upon the name of the Lord shall be saved."

Chapter XII

ELISHA
GREATER IN DEATH THAN IN LIFE

They had put dear Elisha in his coffin, carried him to the cemetery and buried him, and probably had said: "That's the last of him," but it wasn't!

Elisha had passed across the national landscape of Israel's checkered history in an undulating path of light and shadow, dispensing beneficent grace at every step of his journey. The gracious mantle of his master, Elijah, with a double portion of his master's spirit, had been in evidence all along the way. He had befriended the widow, healed the leper, raised a dead child to gladden the heart of its mother, caused the minstrel strains of heavenly melody to echo through the hills, leading a host to triumph and turned a famine into a feast.

Elisha had known what it was to journey on the shady side of life's highway in a path of rude rejection, but he had also heard the plaudits of his people ringing in his ears. He had brought riches to a widow and her two sons, but he had refused wealth for himself offered him from the hand of a cleansed leper. Now the story of his life had all been told, and, like a weaver's shuttle, it had come to the end of the thread, to be silenced forever. So the mourners must have thought when they committed him to burial, but thy were wrong!

RAISED FROM THE DEAD

In 2 Kings 13, two verses tell the unexpected and startling story. "And Elisha died and they buried him and the bands of the Moabites invaded the land at the coming in of the year. And it came to pass as they were burying a man, that, behold they spied a band of men; and they cast the man into the sepulchre of Elisha; and when the man was let down and touched the bones of Elisha, he revived and stood upon his feet."

Is this not most extraordinary? In his lifetime, this man of God had only with great difficulty imparted new life to the dead child as it lay upon the bed. It was only by prostrating himself upon the child face to face, and hands to hands, that Elisha had managed with great difficulty to bring new life into the body of the Shunammite's son. But here the corpse of a man simply touched Elisha's dead bones and the man sprang to life as if by magic.

Surely here is a person greater in his death than he ever was in his life, and in this Elisha is a true type of our Lord Himself who gained His greatest victory on Calvary's Cross and whose illustrious death on the Tree has brought life to spiritually dead sinners in countless millions. Much like Elisha, our Saviour traveled life's highway in beneficent grace. Even as Elisha's name means "Saviour God," it was written of our Lord when He made His humble entrance into this world by way of Bethlehem's manger, "thou shalt call His name Jesus for He shall save His people from their sins," and His name shall be Immanuel, "God with us."

Much like Elisha, too, our Lord traveled the roads of Israel's land, making glad the hearts of widows, filling the empty earthen waterpots with the wine of heavenly joy. What Elisha did for the Shunammite, our Lord did for the woman outside the city of Nain. He raised her boy to gladden her bereaved heart. The Lord Jesus touched the leper who came to Him on the street in Jerusalem and made him clean.

Thus, step by step, there is marked similarity between the pathway of our Lord from the manger to the Cross, and that of Elisha through Israel's land in those days so long ago. Just as Elisha died and was buried, and they thought that was the end of him, so our Saviour was taken and by cruel hands He was slain, and they thought that would be the end of Him. But has it been?

By wicked scheming they brought forth accusations against Jesus, the Lord. They arrayed Him in a purple robe and gave Him a mock trial. They bartered Him at the bar of public opinion on a platform of equality with the notorious and murderous criminal called Barabbas, and the people shouted "away with Him!" They scourged Him, spat in His face, plucked the hair from His cheek, and plaited a crown of cruel thorns and put it upon His blessed brow. Then they led Him up the rugged slope of Golgatha and there on Calvary's hill they crucified Him. After He was slain, a few of His faithful followers begged for His body, and carried it tenderly to the sepulchre, and laid it in the new tomb on which the inexorable power of Rome placed a seal and set a watch, and the world saw Him no more, even as He had said.

That was the last of Him as far as the world is concerned for the record of Scripture would lead us to believe that unbelieving eyes never saw Him again. But was that *the last* of Him?

STILL REMEMBERED

A few days previously, at the evening hour, He had gone with His beloved disciples to an upper room in the city of Jerusalem, and there He had celebrated the Passover feast together with the twelve. He had taken a loaf of bread, and broken it and passed it to them saying, "Take, eat, this is my body which is given for you." Likewise He had taken a cup of wine, a memorial of His shed blood, and there He had instituted the memorial feast declaring: "This do for a remembrance of me." When He died, no doubt the world thought all these things would soon be forgotten.

Twenty centuries have rolled down the course of time, yet week by week in all parts of the world, in every continent and country, literally thousands of His followers assemble together and pledge their allegiance anew to the Christ who died on Calvary. They celebrate this same feast of remembrance, partaking of the loaf that speaks of His body given, and the cup that speaks of His blood shed. And as they do, every eye is on the horizon, watching for the morning star that heralds the coming again of the Saviour. So His death was not the last of Him, for He is remembered lovingly in the hearts of millions throughout the earth today.

MUCH FRUIT

Why do these millions remember Him so warmly and with such affectionate remembrance? Is it because He was a great leader of men whose glamor caught the public eye and gave Him a place of supremacy in the world? No, indeed! Is it because He performed so many miracles in the world, such as giving life to a widow's son, or raising dead Lazarus, or enlarging a scanty store of five loaves and two small fishes into a banquet to feed five thousand men? No, it is not that! Is it because He went about denouncing the Pharisees and showing up the fallacy of their empty religion, putting to shame the paltry hypocrisy of wicked religious leaders? No, it is not that!

The millions who remember Him so affectionately know that there was a day in the life history of each of them when they were like the dead man who was carried by his friends and cast into the tomb of Elisha, and who sprang to life again after touching the prophet's bones. They remember full well that there was a day when they were dead in trespasses and in sins, and then the sweet story of the Cross of Christ carried its golden melody into their hearts, turning their eyes to the Man of the Cross whose life-giving power touched them in their innermost being, and they were born anew. They know the truth of the Scripture, "Except a corn of wheat fall into the ground and die, it abideth alone, but if it die, it bringeth forth much fruit."

This is the grand truth that is mirrored in this final episode in the career of the illustrious Elisha. It is the truth that, before we can have life eternal, another must die in our place and stead. "God commendeth His love toward us in that while we were yet sinners Christ died for us." Not until we appropriate to ourselves the value of the death of Christ can we have new life before God. It is not the *life* of Christ, however wonderful, holy or miraculous that life may be, that brings new life to us. It is His *death*. "He *died* that we might *live*," says the Scripture.

In emphasizing the death of Christ, we do not forget that He is risen from the dead. We seek rather to remind ourselves that the road of our salavtion, the means by which we find peace of heart and conscience before God, is that Christ "was delivered for our offenses, and raised again for our justification." The blessed Man who hung between heaven and earth on Calvary's cruel Tree, who was taken by affectionate hands and placed in Joseph's new tomb, is the same One who on the third day burst the bars of death asunder, and rose triumphant from the grave.

Although unbelievers saw Him no more, His beloved followers knew the exultant joy of being with Him in His resurrection life. They sat at table with Him, they walked the highway with Him, they ate fish and bread together with Him. They handled Him and saw that He was not a spirit, but that He had flesh and bone. Then, after He had been seen by five hundred brethren together at once, a few of them went out yonder to the verdant slopes of Olivet's mountain, and, as they stood around their risen Saviour, He was parted from them. They saw Him go up into the azure blue as His hands were raised in blessing upon their heads, and a cloud received Him out of their sight.

Now he sits on the Father's Throne, exalted at the right hand of God on High where He ever liveth to make intercession for His own. Some day soon He is coming back. He promised: "If I go away I will come again, and receive you unto myself that where I am, there you may be also." This "blessed hope" shines brighter today before the hearts of millions across this sad earth than ever before in all history. "Behold I come quickly," is our Lord's Word to us. We answer back, "Even so come, Lord Jesus."

10/29/11

4/4/18

8/25/20